"The absence of lament in the American Christian church has resulted in a noticeable theological gap and a failure to engage the full breadth and depth of biblical Christian faith. Dr. Rebekah Eklund brings the rigor of academic inquiry balanced with a pastoral heart that offers the necessary corrective to this dysfunctional ecclesial reality. *Practicing Lament* is an important work not only in what it teaches from the depth and integrity of Dr. Eklund's academic work, but also how it is offered, with great sensitivity and spiritual depth. Lament is the spiritual discipline needed by the church and this text offers an essential guide for this long-lost spiritual practice."

—Soong-Chan Rah, author of *Prophetic Lament: A Call for Justice in Troubled Times*

"I can't imagine a more needful book for our time than this one by Rebekah Eklund. So much in our broken world demands to be lamented. Yet because so few of us grew up in families or churches that modeled healthy lament, we need to be trained. Eklund serves here as a theologically skilled, pastorally wise, and immensely helpful guide, training readers in the way of faithful lament—for God's sake and our own!"

—W. David O. Taylor, author of *Open and Unafraid: The Psalms as a Guide to Life*

"Rebekah Eklund has made a powerful case for recovering the worship practice of lament. 'Easter' faith does not cancel out sorrow. And lament is not about giving up on God. It is a cry of anguish reaching out to a personal and trustworthy God. If you are looking to deepen your faith and to walk more fully in the ways of Jesus, Eklund is the perfect guide."

—Nijay K. Gupta, Professor of New Testament, Northern Seminary

"In this warmly written and well-researched book, Professor Eklund invites into the biblical practice of lament. In lament, we join our heartfelt cries with those of the psalmists, the Prophets, and with Jesus himself. As one who has learned the language of lament, I am thankful that this book teaches us how to lament as a healthy spiritual discipline. She also explains how lament helps us engage racial injustice and unrest as well as our global pandemic. This is both a timely and timeless treatment."

—**Douglas Groothuis**, author of *Walking through Twilight: A Wife's Illness—A Philosopher's Lament*

"In this broken time, when nothing is as it should be, Rebekah Eklund invites us to learn and practice the habits of lament as part of a faithful life with God and each other. This little volume is filled with compassion, warmth, and insights that will build up the body of Christ."

—**Stephen Fowl**, Professor of Theology,
Loyola University Maryland

PRACTICING LAMENT

CASCADE COMPANIONS

The Christian theological tradition provides an embarrassment of riches: from Scripture to modern scholarship, we are blessed with a vast and complex theological inheritance. And yet this feast of traditional riches is too frequently inaccessible to the general reader.

The Cascade Companions series addresses the challenge by publishing books that combine academic rigor with broad appeal and readability. They aim to introduce nonspecialist readers to that vital storehouse of authors, documents, themes, histories, arguments, and movements that comprise this heritage with brief yet compelling volumes.

PRACTICING LAMENT

REBEKAH EKLUND

 CASCADE *Books* • Eugene, Oregon

PRACTICING LAMENT

Cascade Companions

Copyright © 2021 Rebekah Eklund. All rights reserved. Except
for brief quotations in critical publications or reviews, no part of
this book may be reproduced in any manner without prior written permission from the publisher. Write: Permissions, Wipf and
Stock Publishers, 199 W. 8th Ave., Suite 3, Eugene, OR 97401.

Cascade Books
An Imprint of Wipf and Stock Publishers
199 W. 8th Ave., Suite 3
Eugene, OR 97401

www.wipfandstock.com

PAPERBACK ISBN: 978-1-7252-7258-3
HARDCOVER ISBN: 978-1-7252-7259-0
EBOOK ISBN: 978-1-7252-7260-6

Cataloguing-in-Publication data:

Names: Eklund, Rebekah, author.

Title: Practicing Lament / by Rebekah Eklund.

Description: Eugene, OR: Cascade Books, 2021 | Series: Cas-
cade Companions | Includes bibliographical references.

Identifiers: ISBN 978-1-7252-7258-3 (paperback) | ISBN 978-1-
7252-7259-0 (hardcover) | ISBN 978-1-7252-7260-6 (ebook)

Subjects: LCSH: Laments in the Bible. | Suffering—Religious
aspects—Christianity. | Bereavement—Religious aspects—
Christianity

Classification: BS1199.L27 E35 2021 (print) | BS1199.L27 (ebook)

Cover art is the painting "Hear My Plea" by artist Rochelle Blumenfeld (https://blumenfeldart.com). The painting is part of a series inspired by the Alvin Ailey American Dance Theater work "Revelations."

For Fritz, Maureen, and Denis

CONTENTS

GRATITUDE

CHRIS SPINKS, MY EDITOR at Cascade Books of Wipf and Stock Publishers, waited patiently for me for a few years until I had the time and space to work on this project. Thank you, Chris, for encouraging me to write this book until I finally did.

Students in my Spring 2020 class "Hope, Death, and the End of the World" helped me to think through the reflections that became the third chapter of this book. When I was wondering how to phrase something in the book, I often thought of how I would explain it to them. Thank you, Jerry, Fatima, Erin, Katherine, Jack, Grace, Enrique, Michelle, Marci, Mark, and Natalie.

Sisters and brothers at my church in Baltimore have shown me examples of what it means to mourn with those who mourn and to rejoice with those who rejoice.

From start to finish, my friend and former Duke ThD colleague Mandy Rodgers-Gates kept me company in online writing retreats as I wrote. I can't imagine how I would have managed to write during a pandemic without her encouragement and virtual presence keeping me on task.

Fritz, Maureen, and Denis adopted me into their family during the 2020 quarantine so that I didn't have to be alone. Out of deep gratitude for their love and care, this book is for them.

INTRODUCTION

WHY LAMENT?

WITH THIS BOOK, I hope to persuade you not only that lament is worth knowing about, but also that it is worth practicing.

My main purpose is to introduce you to lament as a form of prayer, especially in the context of Christianity. Lament is rooted deeply in the Jewish tradition out of which Christianity emerges. Although the Christian tradition has not always been as hospitable to lament, I mean to persuade you that lament is woven deeply into the fabric of the New Testament, and is an essential part of the Christian life. In a faith focused on resurrection hope, patient endurance, and victory in Christ, is there any room for the darkness of our lives? Lament is the prayer that makes that room.

If you're curious about lament and the role that it plays within a particular religious tradition (the diverse Christian traditions), then this book is for you. As a Protestant Christian myself, this book is written from within a Christian tradition and often uses the language of that tradition, but I have endeavored never to be technical or obscure. I've done my best to create a hospitable space for my readers, whether you are Protestant or Catholic or Orthodox, whether you are Jewish or Muslim, or whether you have no religious affiliation at all.

This little book emerges out of a doctoral dissertation that I wrote several years ago about the role of lament in the New Testament. I wrote the dissertation because I wanted to explore a topic that would feel relevant and important to the congregation in Minneapolis where I'd been a pastor. I've always resonated with the prayer of lament in my own life and journey of faith. It became even more personal to me throughout the course of writing it: I lost my mother and my grandfather before I finished, and shortly after I graduated my beloved advisor died.

I haven't reused any material directly from that dissertation or its published form, but the work I did on that project undergirds the thoughts offered here. In that project, I defined lament as "a persistent cry for salvation to the God who promises to save, in a situation of suffering or sin, in the confident hope that this God hears and responds to cries, and acts *now* and *in the future* to make whole. In other words, lament calls upon God to keep God's own promises."[1]

It's a little clunky as a sentence, but on the whole I think it captures what I still think is true about lament. It's a little more cheerful than a definition I might offer today. I'm not so sure that lament is always offered in "confident hope," for example. In fact, I think lament is often offered through clenched teeth and tears, when we're at the end of our rope, when we cling to a thin thread of hope that seems about to snap.

1. Eklund, *Jesus Wept*, 16–17.

Lament is an instinctive act, a deeply human one. It's also, as a specific practice formed within a specific religious tradition, an action that must be learned. Even learning to lament for ourselves can take some practice. The emotions come easily enough; but, it can still take courage to sit long enough with those emotions to know them for what they are, to name them, to imagine what we want in the midst of them, and to see a path forward into a new space.

Likewise lamenting for others, especially those who are different from us, might take some practice. One of the goals of this book is to provide some tools that might make that practice a little easier.

The first chapter lays the groundwork by describing the four-part framework of lament as it appears in the Jewish Scriptures (or what Christians call the Old Testament). The second chapter looks at Jesus' laments in the New Testament. In the third chapter, I explore lament elsewhere in the New Testament, especially in the central Christian prayer (the Lord's Prayer) and the letters of the apostle Paul. The fourth chapter dives deeper into the logic of lament by looking at its twofold function as repentance of sin and protest against injustice. Finally, the fifth chapter offers examples of lament as a form of solidarity and vulnerable hospitality in modern-day communities.

Unless otherwise noted, quotations from Scripture are from the New International Version.

1

TEARING HEAVEN OPEN

> "Oh, that you would rend the heavens and
> come down . . . !" (Isa 64:1)

TEAR OPEN THE HEAVENS and show yourself! Have you ever
made this kind of a fervent plea, hunched over in pain, speaking through tears? I have. It's the cry of those who suffer, who
ache, who fear. It's a cry that begs for God, for *someone* at
least, to show up, to draw near, to be present.

This is the language of lament: a cry for help in the
midst of pain. It's one of the most common forms of prayer
in the Jewish Scriptures, or what Christians call the Old
Testament. Lament appears over and over again in the
book of Psalms, which is sometimes called the prayerbook
or the hymnbook of both Israel and the church. There are
more psalms of lament than any other type of psalm. More
than thanksgiving, more than praise, more than gratitude,
more than moral instruction.

Lament is a defining feature of the vibrant and messy
relationship that Israel has with God. The very name "Israel"

means "the one who wrestles with God." It's a name that comes from the story of Jacob striving all night in a fierce physical contest with an angel, and who, when he emerges wounded but victorious, is given his new name: Israel, the one who strives with God (Gen 32:22–32). Lament is not a polite type of prayer. It's designed for wrestling with God. It's urgent, anguished, demanding. *Come down!*

THE FRAMEWORK OF LAMENT

Lament takes wordless, almost unbearable pain, and gives it a shape and a voice. It provides a structure to hang pain on. Maybe this appeals to me because I'm a person who thrives on routines and schedules. But it also seems true that when everything comes undone, a simple structure can help piece us back together by showing us the way—first this, then that. Step by step through the darkness.

Invocation

The first step of lament is directing the cry somewhere. To whom am I crying out? This is sometimes called the "invocation." We invoke a name; we invoke someone who hears, or someone we hope may hear. In Isa 64:1, the invocation is a gasp of breath; it's just the word "Oh!" Other Old Testament laments appeal to "My God"—*my* God, not just any god but *mine*. In this way, the one who laments claims—and reminds God about—the relationship they've forged. Some laments cry out to the LORD (YHWH), using the divine, unspeakable name that God gave to Moses at the burning bush before sending him to Egypt to rescue God's people (Exod 3:14).

Complaint

The second step is to name what's wrong. This is usually called the "complaint" part of the lament. My heart is broken. I lost a job. I'm lonely. I lost a child or a parent or a friend. I'm afraid. I'm in chronic pain. I long to be married. I'm married but I long to be free of an abusive or life-defeating relationship. Naming what is wrong can be a powerful act. To name something is to know it, which is not always easy. As Joel Willitts writes, "What is not named is not healed."[1]

During the long weeks of social isolation resulting from the coronavirus pandemic in the spring and summer of 2020, I found myself weeping over *everything*—car commercials, news stories about the canceled Olympics, touching stories about pets on social media. I couldn't figure out why I was so fragile (besides the obvious loss of face-to-face relationships).

I sat down one night to pray an examen, a simple prayer that looks back over the day. Where did I feel stress and anxiety today? Where did I experience joy or contentment today? To what is God leading me? As I thought about each question, I realized the real source of my anxiety: I felt utterly helpless. That was my complaint. *I feel so helpless.* There was so much suffering around me—thousands of people dying, millions of people losing their jobs, hospital staff running out of masks and gloves and ventilators, local restaurants and shops closing their doors—and I was floundering, unsure of how to help. Eventually, I would have other complaints. *My beloved colleague is in hospice care and I can't go visit her to say goodbye. I don't know when I will see my family again, or when I will touch another human being again.* Those would come later, piling new pain

1. Willitts, "Following the 'Man of Sorrows,'" 102.

on top of the helplessness. It took courage to give each loss and fear a name, to say it out loud.

For many Old Testament laments, one of the primary complaints is the absence or hiddenness of God. The psalmist often cries out, "Why are you hiding your face from me?" or "Why have you forsaken me?" (Jesus uses this very complaint on the cross, while he is dying.) When things fall apart, when the center does not seem to hold, when the pain seems too great to bear, how could God possibly still be present and paying attention? If God were, surely there would be more light and less suffering. For some lamenters (then and now), the horrifying sense of God's absence or indifference or inexistence is the deepest pain of all.

Many faithful people have struggled with the problem of God's apparent absence. Even Mother Teresa wrote anguished and moving descriptions of her own spiritual desolation: "In the darkness . . . Lord, my God, who am I that You should forsake me? . . . I call, I cling, I want—and there is no One to answer . . ."[2] German pastor Dietrich Bonhoeffer wrestled with God's hiddenness during the dark days of Nazi Germany. He concluded, as he wrote letters to his loved ones from a Nazi prison, that God's powerlessness was paradoxically how God chose to be in solidarity with the suffering of the world. New Testament scholar Dale Allison writes, "I sometimes think the Divinity is like a child who does not know that the game of hide-and-seek is done."[3]

Many parts of Scripture affirm that God's steadfast love for the world never ceases, and that God never departs, even for a moment, from the world that God so loves. Lament is not one of those parts. Lament makes room for the gap between the truth (God never leaves us) and our experience (it sure feels like God does, sometimes).

2. Teresa, *Come Be My Light*, 186–87.

3. Allison, *Luminous Dusk*, 150.

Lament gives a voice to our worst fears and doubts and invites us to say them out loud. It even invites us to speak them to God—even toward a God we may be angry with, or doubtful toward.

Lament sometimes might feel like shouting into the dark. That's what the complaint is for. My mentor Allen Verhey used to say that's what distinguishes lament from despair—even at its bleakest, even when Job curses God and asks to die, lament is still a prayer, which means it still turns toward God, even if it only turns toward God to shake a fist.[4] Job "clings to God against God."[5]

For some people, that might feel liberating; for others, it could feel risky or scandalous to pray that way. That's the gift lament provides; it invites us into a relationship with God where there is real risk—which is what every real relationship always involves. "Biblical faith," says Belden Lane, "is that which limps like Jacob, bearing with it the wounds of its wrestling with God."[6]

Petition

The third step is the plea, or the petition. This is the heart of the lament, its most essential piece. The lamenter requests, or demands, that God act in some way. If one of the common complaints of lament is that God seems to be hidden or sleeping on the job, one of the most frequent pleas is simply for God to be present. Often what I want most when I'm suffering is for someone to be there. One of my favorite biblical images for God is that of an eagle or a mother hen hiding her chicks under her wings (Ps 17:8; Matt 23:37). God's presence is like being sheltered under

4. Verhey, *Christian Art of Dying*, 341.

5. Westermann, "Role of the Lament," 32.

6. Lane, "Hutzpa K'lapei Shamaya," 570.

the warm, protective wings of a fierce mother who would do anything to keep us safe.

Sometimes the lamenter simply asks God to listen. *Hear my cry!* is another common refrain in the psalms. It's easy to rush to speaking when we're with someone who's suffering. We want to offer words of comfort or encouragement or reassurance. Sometimes our words make it better; often they don't. Simply sitting still to listen without interrupting can be a great gift.

I don't normally think of God as a good listener in Scripture. God is the primary speaker in Scripture; God speaks, and the world springs into being. But it's also possible to think about times that God listens in the Bible. In the book of Job, God listens without interrupting to his servant Job hurling complaints at God for thirty-five whole chapters. To be sure, this infuriates Job, who demands that God hear his case—and that is precisely what God does after Job (and Job's unhelpful friends) have had their say.

Similarly, in the book of Lamentations, God's voice is notably absent. The setting of Lamentations is the siege and destruction of the city of Jerusalem, including the temple, and the forced exile of many of the Israelites to live under enemy rule in the Babylonian empire. In the book, several lamenters cry out in pain and anger and profound loss, including the prophet Jeremiah and the city of Jerusalem herself. But God never speaks. Scholars Beau Harris and Carleen Mandolfo suggest, provocatively, that God's silence in the book of Lamentations can be read not as anger or indifference but as "a moment of deep respect for Daughter Zion to pour out her full lament."[7] Perhaps, when God is silent, God is listening.

---

7. Harris and Mandolfo, "Silent God in Lamentations," 141. For different but also lovely reflections on God's silence, see Allison, *Luminous Dusk*, 43–46.

At other times, the plea is for God to act. The petition might be for healing, or help, or rescue from enemies or from death. The petition might be to restore someone's good name after being slandered, or to restore someone to full health after an illness.

Just as it can be revealing to name a complaint, it can be empowering to name a petition. What exactly do I want? What do I need most in the midst of this pain? Sometimes I think the answer is obvious, but then when I try to give voice to a specific request, what I ask for might change. When I realized that one of my complaints was a feeling of helplessness, I wondered what I wanted God to do about that. What was my petition in relation to that particular complaint? I settled on two: 1) pleading with God to take care of the world (the doctors and nurses, the grocery story workers, the migrant farmworkers); and 2) asking God to help me to be faithful with the little corner of the world that was entrusted to me (mainly, at the time, the seventy-two students I was suddenly teaching from a distance).

Trust

The final step is a tricky one, because it's easy to try to brush aside the other steps and head straight for this one. It's even more tempting to urge other people in pain to arrive here as soon as possible. It's the turn toward praise, or hope, or trust. This step is often marked with a "But" or a "Yet." *Yet,* I will trust in you. *But,* I will sing of your steadfast love. The *yet* signals that the person lamenting is still in the midst of their pain, and chooses to trust anyway. Despite the darkness, they reach out in hope. Some people take the turn to praise and hope as evidence that God has answered the lamenter's prayer. I tend to disagree. Lament is a prayer of tensions and contradictions—praising while hurting, hoping while still in the dark. Singing God's praise while still in a foreign land.

I should say right now, before I say more about this fourth step, that these are not neat, sequential steps. This is absolutely crucial. Life is not that tidy. Prayer is not that tidy. We take one step forward and two steps back. In the psalms of lament, the steps occur more than once and often out of order. One might complain, petition, complain again, cry out in hope, petition, and then complain some more. In the book of Lamentations, the affirmation of hope is tucked right into the middle of the book, in chapter 3, and then the complaints continue for another two chapters. The only psalm that neatly follows the framework of lament, more or less step by step and in order, is Psalm 13.

> ¹ How long, Lᴏʀᴅ? Will you forget me forever?
>   How long will you hide your face from me?
> ² How long must I wrestle with my thoughts
>   and day after day have sorrow in my heart?
>   How long will my enemy triumph over me?
> ³ Look on me and answer, Lᴏʀᴅ my God.
>   Give light to my eyes, or I will sleep in death,
> ⁴ and my enemy will say, "I have overcome him,"
>   and my foes will rejoice when I fall.
> ⁵ But I trust in your unfailing love;
>   my heart rejoices in your salvation.
> ⁶ I will sing the Lᴏʀᴅ's praise,
>   for he has been good to me.

You can see the invocation (Lᴏʀᴅ) in verse 1 and again in verse 3 (Lᴏʀᴅ my God). The first two verses offer a series of complaints, marked by the repeated refrain *How long, how long, how long*? The lamenter in this case is identified as King David, and he cries out in anguish or anger over God's apparent absence and the triumph of his enemies. In verses 3–4, we find the petitions, when David pleads with God: *Look on me, answer me, give light to my eyes* (i.e., a request either for wisdom or simply for God to keep him alive). And then at the start of verse 5, you can see the "But" or the "Yet" that marks the turn to praise: "But I trust in your unfailing love," along with a concluding affirmation in verse 6 that the LORD has been good to David.

This psalm is the outlier. All the other lament psalms follow a much more wandering path. (For examples, look at Pss 22 and 69.) And one lament psalm never even makes it to the final step. Psalm 88 begins and ends in darkness.

Psalm 88 is ascribed to a man named Heman the Ezrahite. Heman begins by invoking God's sacred name and God's power to save: "LORD, you are the God who saves me" (v. 1). He then offers a plea: "turn your ear to my cry" (v. 3). And then Heman describes his pain:

> I am overwhelmed with troubles
>   and my life draws near to death.
> I am counted among those who go down to the
> pit;
>   I am like one without strength.
> I am set apart with the dead,
>   like the slain who lie in the grave,
> whom you remember no more,
>   who are cut off from your care. (Ps 88:3–5)

Heman goes on to complain that although he cries every day to the LORD, God has rejected him and has hidden God's face. Here is Heman's last line:

> You have taken from me friend and neighbor—
>   darkness is my closest friend. (Ps 88:18)

There is no "Yet" in this lament. Heman never makes the turn to praise, to hope, or to trust. Perhaps he can't see that far through the darkness.

I think it is beautiful that Ps 88 is in Scripture. Its inclusion in the Bible is a source of enormous encouragement to me. This, *this*, is an authorized prayer for the faithful. This prayer is for me and for you when we can't yet find our way out of the darkness and into the light. Including Ps 88 in the book of Psalms says that it is acceptable to cry out in fear and pain and rage and never make it all the way to praise. God receives those laments, too.

Perhaps God treasures those prayers most of all. After all, God too knows what it's like to sit in the darkness and pray anguished tears, because God has tasted the bitterness (and the joys) of being human. Because Jesus sat and wept in the darkness in a garden called Gethsemane, so did God. Because Jesus cried out in lament while he was dying on a cross, wondering if his Father had abandoned him, so did God.[8]

There's one final thing to observe about Ps 88: the psalm itself has companions. That is, when the psalms were eventually collected and arranged in the book of Psalms, they were grouped into five sections and placed in a certain order. Psalm 88 is bounded on one side by Ps 87, a song of joy over Zion, and on the other by Ps 89, a hymn of exultant

---

8. This is sometimes called the "communication of idioms," or the "communication of properties." It's a daring claim that we cannot speak of Christ's humanity and Christ's divinity in two tidy, separate columns. What is true of Jesus the human is true of God the Son. This leads to a welter of seemingly paradoxical statements like "God laments" and "God died" and "God [the Son] felt abandoned by God [the Father]." Of course, the Christian tradition places some boundaries around these claims. Most Christian traditions insist that God *as God* did not die. One member of the Trinity was not snuffed out temporarily when Jesus died on the cross. See the discussion in González, *Mañana*, 109–11.

praise in God's steadfast love. This psalm is darkness embraced with joy and hope.

To be sure, Ps 89 itself turns to lament in its final lines, crying out to God to fulfill God's promises to save Israel by redeeming them out of their exile (vv. 38–51). It's a lament that asks God to act in accordance with God's own character. God is a God of faithfulness—then, be faithful! God is a God of mercy—show mercy! God is a God of justice—let justice roll down! Ethan the Ezrahite, the psalmist of Ps 89, concludes in the way that his fellow Ezrahite Heman cannot: with praise ("Blessed be the LORD forever"), which is the last line of Book Four of the book of Psalms.

The community honors Heman's prayer by allowing it to end in darkness. Nobody insisted that Heman add a "But"; nobody violated his grief by adding a line of praise to his psalm later. But the community also made sure that this section of their prayer book ends collectively in blessing and not in despair. When we can't get ourselves to hope, the community of faith or friendship can get there for us.

Kathryn Greene-McCreight makes a similar point about those who suffer from mental illness. She uses the last line of Ps 88 as the title for her book *Darkness Is My Only Companion*, a book in which she explores her own experience as a Christian with a mental illness. "This is why we need the scriptures and the community of faith," she writes. "They contribute faith and hope to us as from a well that cannot be reached from the depths of mental illness."[9]

GOD BREAKS THE SILENCE

Just a little earlier in the chapter, I claimed that God remains silent in the book of Lamentations. The Israelites lament in anguish, but God never responds. This is true

9. Greene-McCreight, *Darkness Is My Only Companion*, 124.

in Lamentations itself but is perhaps not true if one looks at the prophetic companions of Lamentations, especially Isaiah. It's possible to read portions of the biblical book of Isaiah as a direct response to the complaints in Lamentations. Through the prophet Isaiah, God demonstrates that God has heard the suffering of God's people and will respond to their petitions.

For example, Jewish tradition pairs the reading of Lamentations with selections from the book of the prophet Isaiah (chs. 40–63). Lamentations is the assigned reading for the service on the eve of the holiday called Tisha b'Av (the Ninth of Av), which is a holy day commemorating the greatest tragedies in Jewish history, including the destruction of the two temples in Jerusalem.[10] The assigned Scripture readings for the seven weeks following Tisha b'Av draw from Isaiah, and they "chart a process of reconciliation and consolation in which God deploys a wide range of strategies to console Israel and bring her back into relationship."[11]

Like the embrace of Ps 88 by its joyful and hopeful companions (Pss 87 and 89), Lamentations is given its own space but is not left alone; it is not the final word. The Jewish tradition of reading Isaiah's hopeful reassurances after Lamentations' despair "allows liturgical space for the sorrow and despair of Lamentations to be expressed without being crushed by the premature arrival of 'good news.' Yet, at the same time, it does not allow Lamentations the last word. In this way lament and rejoicing [are] held in balance and in place."[12]

The prophet Jeremiah is traditionally identified as the author of Lamentations. Either he or a nameless lamenter opens the book with the poignant cry, "How lonely sits the

10. Av is a month in the Jewish calendar.

11. Stern, "Lamentations in Seasonal Context."

12. Parry, "Wrestling with Lamentations," 129.

city that once was full of people!" (Lam 1:1). Five times in chapter 1 alone, Jeremiah (or the unnamed mourner) complains that Jerusalem has no one to comfort her (Lam 1:2, 9, 16, 17, 21).

Isaiah chapter 40 opens with God commanding his prophet Isaiah, "Comfort my people!" (Isa 40:1). Over and over again throughout the book of Isaiah, God promises comfort for Israel (Isa 12:1; 40:1; 49:13; 51:3, 12; 52:9; 57:18; 61:2; 66:11, 13). Lamentations and Isaiah use the same word for comfort (in Hebrew, *nicham*; in the Greek version, *parakaleō*).

At the end of Lamentations, the narrator speaks in the collective voice of all Israel, asking God, "Why do you forget us forever?" (Lam 5:20). God quotes this line back to Israel in Isaiah 49: "Zion said, 'The Lord has forsaken me, the Lord has forgotten me.'" God goes on to insist that this is impossible: "Can a mother forget the baby at her breast and have no compassion on the child she has borne? Though she may forget, I will not forget you!" (Isa 49:14–15). Even if a mother were to forget her own baby (an almost unthinkable proposition), God could never forget the people whom God loves as God's own child (Hos 11:1–11). In the last chapter of Isaiah, God promises to comfort Israel the way a mother comforts her children (Isa 66:13).

By contrast, the very last line of Lamentations ends on a note that is almost as bleak as the end of Psalm 88. The second-to-last verse offers a petition: "Restore us to yourself, Lord" (Lam 5:21), but then the narrator hesitates, and adds, "unless you have utterly rejected us and are angry with us beyond measure" (Lam 5:22).[13] The book ends there, on this uncertain and unresolved note. (In fact, it is Jewish tradition today not to end a reading of Lamentations

---

13. Some English translations are even bleaker: "But thou hast utterly rejected us; thou art very wroth against us" (KJV).

at verse 22, but instead to repeat verse 21 one more time to conclude the reading.)[14]

This tension isn't resolved until Isa 54, when God responds to Lamentations' final anxious petition by re-assuring Israel that God's momentary anger was quickly overcome by God's mercy: "In overflowing wrath for a moment I hid my face from you, but with everlasting love I will have compassion on you, says the LORD, your Re-deemer" (Isa 54:8).

Reading books for their own narrative integrity is a good practice. Just as we shouldn't leap too quickly to the "hope and praise" stage of the lament, we should resist the temptation to allow Isaiah to resolve all of Lamentations' pain too neatly. Listen respectfully and in solidarity with the wounded and outraged voices of Lamentations' victims. Sit awhile in silence with them.

Then and only then, because Scripture is a unified whole, and the biblical canon has bound Lamentations and Isaiah together into one book, we can hear Isaiah complet-ing the turn to praise, what the lamenters of Jerusalem wonder if they'll ever be able to do. We hear God respond-ing to Israel's lament with reassurances of steadfast love and promises of comfort.

DIVINE COMPASSION

Some scholars even propose that it is lament that moves God to action in Scripture. Old Testament scholar James Kugel, for example, argues that the cry of the suffering provokes the divine response. The cry of the victim "is, par

14. Likewise, Elsie Stern points out that the Jewish liturgical tra-dition embeds the reading of Lamentations "within a larger cycle that is ultimately redemptive and reconciliatory" (Stern, "Lamentations in Seasonal Context").

excellence, the thing that humans do that makes God act. . . . I am powerless *not* to react, God seems to say, once the abused party cries out to Me."[15]

In the book of Exodus, "the Israelites groaned in their slavery and cried out, and their cry for help because of their slavery went up to God" (Exod 2:23). When YHWH hears their groaning, the LORD remembers the covenant with Israel and is moved to act; the next thing that happens is that God appears to Moses in a burning bush, and commissions him to journey to Egypt to rescue God's people.

Rachel offers another example. In the Old Testament, Rachel is a woman of multiple sorrows: she is usurped by her older sister Leah, who marries the man she loves; she endures years of childlessness while watching her sister give birth again and again; and once she does get pregnant, she dies in childbirth. Her final act is to name her son Ben-Oni, "son of my sorrow" (a name her husband quickly erases, renaming her son Ben-Jamin, "son of my right hand") (Gen 35:16–20).

When Rachel next appears in the Old Testament, she is still weeping. The Lord declares to his prophet Jeremiah that Rachel's voice is still heard in Ramah, "mourning and great weeping, Rachel weeping for her children and refusing to be comforted, because they are no more" (Jer 31:15). Ramah is a town belonging to the tribe of Benjamin, invoking Rachel's sorrowful memory of her son, but it was also a gathering place of the Israelites bound in chains, on their way to exile in Babylon after the overthrow of Jerusalem and the destruction of the temple (Jer 40:1).

God responds to Rachel in the immediately following verses: "This is what the Lord says: 'Restrain your voice from weeping and your eyes from tears, for your work will

15. Kugel, *God of Old*, 120, 110; see also Ellington, *Risking Truth*, 177.

be rewarded,' declares the Lord. 'They will return from the land of the enemy. . . . Your children [the exiled Jews] will return to their own land'" (Jer 31:16–17). God has heard and responded to her wailing with a promise of hope and restoration.

Later Jewish tradition mused over why it was Rachel's weeping that moved God to forgive Israel and bring them home from exile. A Jewish commentary (a.k.a. a midrash) on the book of Lamentations portrays God grieving over Jerusalem's destruction and the exile of God's people. At God's bidding, the prophet Jeremiah summons Abraham, Isaac, Jacob, and Moses from their graves to lament Jerusalem's destruction. One by one, they plead for God to have mercy and restore the people. Finally, Rachel approaches God, and explains that she helped her sister Leah deceive Jacob on their wedding night (tricking him into thinking it was Rachel he was marrying, and not Leah) out of love for her sister. Only then does God relent and promise to restore Israel.[16]

In another midrash, the same patriarchs appear before God when summoned, but instead of lamenting, they blame God for the destruction of Jerusalem. Abraham reminds God that God stopped him from killing his son Isaac; why couldn't God similarly stop the Babylonians from destroying Jerusalem? Scholar Frederick Niedner continues the story: "Similarly, Moses asks why God couldn't save Jerusalem just as the children of Israel had been rescued from Pharaoh at the Red Sea. All of them reproach God and no one mourns with God until Rachel arrives. She says little and blames no one. She simply weeps inconsolably." Again, it is Rachel's grief that moves God. "There is hope for your future," God tells her. "Your children shall come back to their own country."[17]

16. *Midrash Rabbah Lamentations*, Proem XXIV.

17. Niedner, "Rachel's Lament," 410–11, citing Ginzberg, *Legends*

One final Jewish tradition—this time from the Jewish mystical tradition known as Kabbalah—teaches that God will send the Messiah in response to Rachel's weeping, and that the Messiah will be crowned at Rachel's grave in Ramah. His first act will be to comfort her.[18]

In the Gospel of Matthew, Rachel appears one more time, once again weeping and refusing to be comforted. This time, she weeps for all the baby boys slaughtered by Herod in his murderous pursuit of the one born to be King of the Jews (Matt 2:16–18). Rachel's weeping occurs just before John the Baptist's announcement that "the kingdom of heaven has come near" and his quotation of Isaiah's instruction to "Prepare the way for the Lord" (Matt 3:2, 3; quoting Isa 40:3). And two chapters later, at the beginning of his ministry, Jesus promises that those who mourn will be comforted (Matt 5:4). The Messiah arrives—again in response to Rachel's tears.

Sometimes we might feel like Rachel, bearing the weight of many losses, weeping and refusing to be consoled. What could possibly comfort us when we have lost a child, or a cherished dream, or a friend who made us whole, when the world seems too broken to mend? Sometimes we are in the grief of Lamentations and wonder if there will ever be a response. The petitions of lament might remain unanswered.

There are many helpful theological approaches to the problem of unanswered prayer. Lament is not one of them. It doesn't try to resolve the puzzle or the pain of petitions that seem to go unheard. Instead, it envelops even that pain, and lifts it back to God in complaint, and in hope that God listens.

---

of the Bible, 628–31.

18. Niedner, "Rachel's Lament," 411. For the tradition that the Messiah will arrive and be crowned at Ramah, see *Zohar* 2.7–9, in Dresner, *Rachel*, 204–5.

REFLECTION

1. Could you use the four-part framework of the lament prayer to write your own lament?

2. Why is it important to stay with suffering, or complaint, and not move too quickly to praise?

3. Does it seem true that God is especially moved to action by suffering? Why or why not?

2

JESUS WEPT

"Jesus wept." (John 11:35)

LAMENT IN THE NEW TESTAMENT?

IN THE FIRST CHAPTER, I explored how lament appears over and over throughout the Jewish Scripture and is a central part of God's relationship with Israel. But what about the New Testament? At first glance, it looks like there's less lament in the New Testament. There are no psalms; there's no book of Lamentations. The most catastrophic event in the New Testament—the crucifixion of Jesus—is narrated not as cause for grief but as God's triumph over sin, death, and evil.

In fact, sometimes it might seem as if there's no lament at all after Jesus' resurrection. If God has won, is there anything left to complain about? Christian traditions have not always embraced lament, protest, or complaint toward God. Some Christians have worried that these types of prayers represent a lack of faith or might even be a sinful form of rebellion against God's perfect will.

In the next few chapters, I'll try to persuade you not only that there is lament in the New Testament, but that lament is an indispensable part of the life of faith. Lament is woven deeply into the Christian way—"the Way" being one of the earliest nicknames for being a Christian. So where *does* lament appear in the New Testament? It appears first and foremost on the lips of Jesus.

JESUS CRIES FOR THE SUFFERING OF A CITY HE LOVES

The Gospel writers give us only occasional glimpses into Jesus' emotions. They're ancient biographers, not modern writers; for the most part, they're not interested in exploring the inner lives of their characters. When they do open up a window, it makes us pay attention. They tell us, for example, that Jesus had compassion on the crowds. He was moved by their needs, their hunger, their sickness. The verb, "had compassion," literally means "to be moved in the bowels"—that is, to have a powerful, visceral response. (Modern thinkers tend to locate emotions like love and pity in the heart; ancient thinkers located such emotions in the intestines.) The Gospels don't record Jesus' laughter for us (although I like to think of him laughing with his disciples). But they do report that Jesus cried.

Jesus cries at least twice in the Gospels. Once, he weeps at the grave of a friend. (I'll talk about that episode in chapter 4; it's hugely important, but it's not really an example of Jesus lamenting.) And, he weeps over the city of Jerusalem, crying out, "Jerusalem, Jerusalem, you who kill the prophets and stone those sent to you, how often I have longed to gather your children together, as a hen gathers her chicks under her wings, and you were not willing. Look, your house is left to you desolate" (Matt 23:37–38; see also Luke 13:34–35).

His mourning for the city is a specific kind of lament. It actually has the characteristics of two different types of lament: a dirge and a prophetic or intercessory lament.

The Dirge

Dirges are funeral songs. In the ancient world, dirges were sung for cities as well as for people. If one wants to be precise, dirges aren't technically laments (the way I'm defining them in this book), because they're not always prayers, and there's usually no petition or request. A dirge is simply sorrow over a loss. It's the sorrowful complaint of the lament form without the other parts. When the godly king Josiah died, the prophet Jeremiah composed dirges for the Israelites to sing for Josiah, so that all the people of Israel could mourn his passing (2 Chr 35:25). In the book of Revelation, an angel sings a dirge over the prophesied fall of "Babylon the great," which was a thinly veiled metaphor for the powerful city of Rome (Rev 18). Of course, this is a dirge with an ironic edge: Babylon/Rome is depicted as the great enemy of God, and its downfall is celebrated as a divine victory over the forces of oppression, greed, and idolatry. Still, the angel's song in Rev 18 is recognizable as a dirge ("Fallen, fallen, is Babylon the great!").

When the angel sings his mournful song over Babylon/Rome, it's the end of the first century and Rome is still standing strong, at the height of its powers. The dirge anticipates a fall that has not yet happened. Similarly, when Jesus speaks his mournful words over Jerusalem, in approximately AD 30, the destruction of the city (by Rome!)

is four decades in the future. Yet he looks ahead and sees the suffering to come.

In Luke's Gospel, Jesus pauses to weep a second time over Jerusalem just before he enters the city one last time, in the final week of his life. As he weeps, he says, "The days will come upon you when your enemies will build an embankment against you and encircle you and hem you in on every side. They will dash you to the ground, you and the children within your walls. They will not leave one stone on another" (Luke 19:43–44a). Unlike Revelation's triumphant dirge, this is a song of sorrow.

Prophetic Lament: Intercession

But Jesus does not merely (or even primarily) sing a dirge over Jerusalem's eventual fall. He steps into the role of a prophet and mourns over God's coming judgment. The basic role of a prophet in Israel was to be a messenger—to bring God's words to the people. Sometimes, the prophet also brought the people's words back to God. Sometimes the prophet "stood in the breach" between the people and God, representing them, pleading their case. Standing in the breach meant trying to repair the breach by urging the people to repent and turn back to God. But it also meant wrestling with God, hoping to protect the people from God's anger—and that's when the prophet often turns to lament to make his case. In the book of Ezekiel, God notes (perhaps with sorrow) that God looked for someone to "stand before me in the gap on behalf of the land so I would not have to destroy it, but I found no one" (Ezek 22:30).[1]

Abraham fulfills the role of the lamenting intercessor when he bargains with God over the fate of the city of

1. Widmer, *Moses, God*, 103–6. See also Schroeder, "'Standing in the Breach,'" 16–23.

Sodom, asking if God might consider sparing the city for a certain number of people—a number that grows smaller and smaller as Abraham probes to see how low God is willing to go (Gen 18:17–33). God first considers hiding the plan to destroy the city from Abraham, but decides not to; instead, God seems to invite Abraham to prompt God to reconsider (Gen 18:17). Perhaps, scholar Terence Fretheim writes, the question of justice for the city "is God's agenda before it is Abraham's."[2]

Moses fulfills the same role when he tries to persuade God not to destroy or abandon Israel out of anger. When Israel breaks the first two commandments (immediately after receiving them) by making a golden calf and worshipping it, God is furious, but rather than punishing them right away, God goes to Moses first. The Lord tells Moses, "Now leave me alone so that my anger may burn against them and that I may destroy them" (Exod 32:10). (This is a bit like seeking out somebody who's sitting in the next room minding their own business, and demanding, "Leave me alone!") Perhaps, Michael Widmer suggests, "YHWH seeks to 'provoke' Moses to prayerfully subvert His plan to destroy Israel."[3]

Moses, like Abraham, steps into the breach. He pleads with God to turn away from anger, pointing out that God did not go to all the trouble of rescuing these people from Egypt just to destroy them, and reminding God of the covenant promises (Exod 32:11–13). Immediately, "the Lord relented and did not bring on his people the disaster he had threatened" (Exod 32:14).

Are these laments? In a way. They overlap with the fourfold pattern of lament we looked at in chapter 1 (invocation, complaint, petition, trust). The intercessor calls

2. Fretheim, *Suffering of God*, 49.

3. Widmer, *Moses, God*, 348.

upon God (face to face, in this case!). He then presents the complaint, which is usually about the severity of God's punishment, held up to the light of God's character as a just and merciful God. Finally, the prophet petitions God to forgive and relent from punishing.

Remarkably, God hopes and even expects that the prophet will intercede for Israel so that God may exercise mercy: "God allows the prophet to represent in his prayer His own attribute of mercy."[4] The runaway prophet Jonah is the perfect example of what happens when the prophetic mediator fails to fulfill his intercessory role: God makes sure the prophet fulfills his role whether he likes it or not. This type of lament suggests our laments are not only on our own behalf, but are also for the sake of others—a theme I'll return to in chapter 5.

What does all this have to say about Jesus weeping over Jerusalem? Jesus doesn't appear to be stepping into the role of the intercessor, because he makes no plea for God to avert judgment and spare Jerusalem. Later, he will intercede on behalf of the people who crucified him, asking his Father to forgive them (Luke 23:34). But here it seems that the fate of Jerusalem is sealed, and Jesus weeps over the certainty of their destruction and mourns the chance they once had to turn aside God's judgment. In this moment, Jesus is less like Abraham and Moses and more like another prophet: Jeremiah.

In the book of Jeremiah, God repeatedly has to instruct the prophet *not* to intercede on behalf of the people, which suggests Jeremiah naturally would have taken on this role (Jer 7:16; 11:14; 14:11; 15:1; 16:5–9). So Jeremiah laments instead. In a line made famous in an African American spiritual, Jeremiah cries out, "Is there no balm in Gilead?" (The region of Gilead was well-known for its

4. Muffs, *Love and Joy*, 33.

medicinal balms and ointments.) "Is there no physician there? Why then is there no healing for the wound of my people?" (Jer 8:22).

It's actually hard at this point to tell who is crying out: Jeremiah or God. The phrase "my people" is claimed by both speakers. Jeremiah (or God) goes on, "Oh, that my head were a spring of water and my eyes a fountain of tears! I would weep day and night for the slain of my people" (Jer 9:1). The prophet's grief mingles with God's grief, as they mourn together over God's judgment of the elect people. Yes, it is affirmed as a just judgment, brought on by their continual idolatry, lies, slander, and refusal to turn back to God (Jer 9:2–6). Still God and Jeremiah cry out in grief over the people's suffering and their coming destruction at the hands of Babylon.

Jesus' weeping over Jerusalem is like this. It expresses the grief of Jesus (and God) over Jerusalem's unwilling-ness to accept Jesus as her true prophet, and over the ruthless destruction of the holy city by the Roman army forty years after Jesus' lament. When Jesus laments over Jerusalem's unwillingness to be gathered "under his wings" (Matt 23:37; Luke 13:34), he invokes a biblical metaphor for God's sheltering love and protection. The image of God sheltering the people of Israel under divine wings oc-curs repeatedly throughout the Old Testament (e.g., Deut 32:11–12; Ruth 2:12). After David fled and hid in a cave to escape King Saul, who was trying to kill him, David declared to God, "I will take refuge in the shadow of your wings until the disaster has passed" (Ps 57:1). One of my favorite verses has always been the psalmist's cry, "Because you are my help, I sing in the shadow of your wings" (Ps 63:7; see also Pss 17:8; 36:7; 61:4; 91:4).

Jesus' longing to gather the people of Jerusalem under his wings—and his complaint, his lament, that they refuse to be gathered—reflects God's longing to shelter and protect God's people. Divine and prophetic grief mingle. "If in these days you—even you—had known the things that make for peace!" (Luke 19:42).

So the first way that Jesus laments in the New Testament is as a prophet, whose role is not only to deliver God's messages to the people but also to intercede with God on behalf of the people when they have strayed. The next way he laments is more personal: he suffers from the fear of death.

JESUS FACES HIS OWN DEATH

The first time I felt the sting of my own mortality, I was twenty-five. I had just been diagnosed with a handful of multisyllabic medical issues, including osteoporosis and an endocrine disorder that is considered a genetic cancer (not because it gave me cancer, but because it put me at risk for a variety of cancers). I came face to face with the truth we all eventually confront: all of us will die. At twenty-five, I was forced to reconsider the strength of my hope in the resurrection, in my belief that even in death God would hold me in God's hands and never let me go. Even in light of that hope, I lived for awhile under the dark shadow of fear. Paul surely knew the weight of that fear when he described death as an enemy, and declared that death is the last enemy whom God destroys in the end (1 Cor 15:26).

Jesus also, according to the Gospels, knew the weight of that fear. The night before he died, he gathered with his disciples to eat one last meal, a Passover Seder. He knows that he's about to undergo betrayal, suffering, and death. Three times, he's warned his disciples this moment was coming. Now it's almost here. After singing the final hymn of the Seder, Jesus goes with his disciples to a garden called

Gethsemane, on a hill called the Mount of Olives across the valley from the city (Matt 26:36–46; Mark 14:32–42; Luke 22:39–46).

He asks his three closest followers (Peter, James, and John) to walk a little farther into the garden with him, and he begins to be deeply distressed, sorrowful, troubled, and anguished (as variously described in Matt 26:37; Mark 14:33; and Luke 22:44). This is the language of a lamenter, of a person in pain preparing to cry out to God (e.g., Pss 6:3; 31:10; 42:6). Jesus tells his companions, "My soul [*psychē*] is overwhelmed with sorrow to the point of death" (Matt 26:38; Mark 14:34).

The word for "overwhelmed with sorrow" is the Greek word *perilypos* (very sad, or exceedingly sad). These two words—*psychē* and *perilypos*—are faint but tantalizing echoes of the Greek version of a lament psalm: "Why are you exceedingly sad [*perilypos*], my soul [*psychē*]?" asks the troubled singer of Ps 42.[5] "My tears have been my food day and night, while people say to me all day long, 'Where is your God?'" (Ps 42:3, 5, 6). In the garden of Gethsemane, as Jesus faces the prospect of his betrayal and a painful death, he uses the language of lament to express his fear and grief.

Then, Jesus throws himself facedown onto the ground in sorrow and distress and begins to pray.[6] Even this most famous of prayers has the shape of a lament. It begins with a personal invocation, "*Abba*, Father"—Jesus calling on the close, familial relationship he has with God. He's already expressed a complaint ("My soul is overwhelmed with sorrow to the point of death"). Now we hear a petition: "Take

5. The psalm, of course, was originally in Hebrew. The New Testament writers, including the Gospel writers, were familiar with the Greek version of the Old Testament, known as the Septuagint.

6. In Luke's version, he kneels. John's Gospel lacks an account of Jesus' prayer in the garden.

this cup from me." He asks God to remove the cup of his suffering. Like any human being, Jesus doesn't want to die. But then Jesus speaks one small word: "Yet." He goes on, "Yet not what I will, but what you will" (Mark 14:36). Like so many lamenters, he makes the turn to trust, placing himself in his Father's hands.

Once he finishes his lament and picks himself up from the ground, brushing the dirt from his clothes, he hands himself over to the gathering darkness—betrayed by a close friend, denied by another, arrested by night, tried on false charges, beaten and mocked, and executed as a criminal by the empire that rules over his people. Before he dies, he will cry out in lament again.

JESUS LAMENTS AS HE DIES

The last words Jesus speaks are words of lament. This is true in its own way in all four Gospels, but it's most obvious in Matthew and Mark.

My God, Why Have You Forsaken Me? (Psalm 22)

In the first two Gospels, as Jesus is dying on the cross, he cries out, "My God, my God, why have you forsaken me?" (Matt 27:46; Mark 15:34). Both Gospel writers preserve the original Aramaic of the cry: "*Eloi, Eloi, lema sabachthani?*" (Aramaic is an ancient language related to Hebrew; it's likely the main language that Jesus and his disciples spoke.)

Jesus' cry is a quotation of the first line of a lament psalm, Ps 22. The psalmist goes on, "Why are you so far from saving me, so far from my cries of anguish? My God, I cry out by day, but you do not answer, by night, but I find no rest" (Ps 22:1b–2). The rest of the psalm alternates back and forth between praise ("Yet you are enthroned as the

Holy One"), complaints ("All who see me mock me"), and petitions ("Do not be far from me"). Multiple details from this psalm make their way into the description of Jesus' crucifixion—the mocking bystanders, casting lots for Jesus' clothes. This lament psalm is the constant background music to Jesus' final hours.

Into Your Hands (Psalm 31)

In Luke's Gospel, by contrast, Jesus' final words seem calm and confident. He intercedes even for the people who condemned him to death, asking God to forgive them (Luke 23:34). He reassures another criminal being crucified with him that they will be together in Paradise (Luke 23:43). And, finally, Jesus cries out in a loud voice, "Father, into your hands I commit my spirit" (Luke 23:46). This does not sound at all like a lament. But it's actually a quotation from a different lament psalm, Psalm 31. It's simply from a trusting portion of the lament. In the psalm, it's followed immediately by a petition: "deliver me, LORD, my faithful God" (Psalm 31:5b). A few verses later, the same psalmist cries out:

> Be merciful to me, LORD, for I am in distress;
> my eyes grow weak with sorrow,
> my soul and body with grief.
> My life is consumed by anguish
> and my years by groaning;
> my strength fails because of my affliction,
> and my bones grow weak.
> Because of all my enemies,
> I am the utter contempt of my neighbors
> and an object of dread to my closest friends—
> those who see me on the street flee from me.
> I am forgotten as though I were dead;

> I have become like broken pottery.
> For I hear many whispering,
>   "Terror on every side!"
> They conspire against me
>   and plot to take my life. (Ps 31:9–13)

Suddenly this sounds much more like the scene at Golgotha, where Jesus is being crucified. In that context, the cry "Into your hands I commit my spirit" sounds a lot more like Jesus facedown in the dirt in Gethsemane, in anguish, sweating blood, and still finding the courage to say, "Yet not my will but yours be done." The Reformer John Calvin understood these last words in Luke in exactly that way. Calvin knew Ps 31 well, and he wrote, "There is no doubt that Christ, in the anguish of the temptations that beset Him, let out this cry at last with a deep and burning effort."[7]

Jesus Thirsts (Psalm 42, Psalm 69)

That leaves John's account of Jesus' final moments. In John's Gospel, Jesus' final two sayings aren't quotations of lament psalms, but they do have their own links to the prayer of lament. Just before he dies, he says, "I am thirsty." It's a surprisingly practical, even prosaic, thing to say. Of course he's thirsty. Soldiers and guards usually don't pay much attention to the comfort of their prisoners. He's probably been thirsty for hours or even since the day before. And now he's been hanging on a cross for hours under the sun, slowly dying.

John calls attention over and over to Jesus' real human body, his flesh and bones and now his dry mouth. The Word became *flesh*. The Word got tired. The Word asked a woman, a despised outsider, for a drink of water on a hot afternoon.

7. Calvin, *Harmony of the Gospels*, 210.

Now the Word, who once promised that same woman living water, is thirsty. The Living Water thirsts.

Thirst is also, simultaneously, a common metaphor in Scripture, especially in the laments. The psalmist thirsts for the presence of the living God. To thirst for God means to long for God, to feel the lack or absence of God.

In Ps 42, which Jesus borrows from when he prays in Gethsemane, the psalmist's soul "thirsts for God" (Ps 42:2). In Ps 22, which Jesus quotes from the cross (in Mark and Matthew), the psalmist writes, "my tongue is glued to my throat" (Ps 22:15). And in Ps 69, another lament psalm, the lamenter complains that he found nobody to comfort him, and that instead of helping him, "They . . . gave me vinegar for my thirst" (Ps 69:21)—which is exactly what the bystanders do for Jesus after he says he's thirsty (John 19:29).

It Is Finished (Psalm 22?)

Last of all, Jesus simply says, "It is finished" (John 19:30). Like his final word in Luke, this sounds like a triumphant or confident declaration. Perhaps John's Gospel simply doesn't portray Jesus as speaking lament with his final words, as the other three Gospels do.

When I first began exploring the role of lament in the New Testament, I read Ps 22 over and over again. That psalm made it deep into my bones. And I began to wonder if Jesus' cry "It is finished" is the faintest echo of the last line of Ps 22: "[God] has done it!" Perhaps John's Gospel completes the pattern of lament that Mark and Matthew begin. I can't prove that to you, but it strikes me as a lovely way to hear the laments of Jesus, which begin (in canonical order) with Jesus' despairing quotation of Ps 22's first verse in Matthew's Gospel, and concludes with Ps 22's last line, its trusting cry of praise spoken by Jesus in the Fourth Gospel just before he draws his final breath.

This way of thinking about Jesus' final words brings the missing element of trust from the lament pattern into Mark and Matthew, but it also insists that the element of complaint and petition be brought into Luke and John. The invoking of a relationship, a cry of grief and despair, a sense of divine abandonment, an urgent plea for help, a declaration of trust and praise in the midst of the deepest suffering—the fullness of lament is there in Jesus' final hour.

EMBODIED LAMENTS: JESUS HEARS AND HEALS

There's one other way that lament makes an appearance in the four Gospel accounts of Jesus' life. Jesus cries out in lament himself, but he's also on the receiving end of some laments in the Gospels. We might consider these embodied laments, or narrative enactments of the pattern of lament.[8]

"Have mercy on me!" people cry out to Jesus over and over again in the Gospels. Their complaints are many. They or their children or their friends are sick. They or their children or their friends have been seized by evil powers who won't let go. They are hungry. They are blind. They are outcasts who haven't been touched by another human being in years.

This is a cry we also hear in the psalms, directed to God. "Have mercy on me!" a person in pain prays over and over again.

> Give me relief from my distress; have mercy on me. (Ps 4:1)

8. O'Day, "Surprised by Faith," 290–301; Ebner, "Klage und Auferweckungshoffnung," 81–86.

> Have mercy on me, LORD, for I am faint; heal
> me, LORD. (Ps 6:2; see also Ps 41:4)

> Have mercy and lift me up from the gates of
> death. (Ps 9:13)

The complaints in the Psalms are also many. Their enemies
surround and pursue them. They are sick or faint or close
to death. They stagger under the burdens of their sins and
long to be free. In the Psalms, these cries for mercy are lifted
to God, but no narrative tells us how God replies, even if
the psalmist might express his hope in God's mercy.

When people cry out to Jesus for mercy in the Gospels,
he always hears and responds with compassion. He never
ignores them or sends them away or tells them to stop complaining. He heals them and their children and their friends.
Sometimes he commends them for their faith. Sometimes
he just heals them. Jesus restores their sight and lifts up the
bent-over and frees them from their burdens.

Once, the disciples get caught out in a fierce storm on
the Sea of Galilee. Jesus, who must be a sound sleeper, was
sleeping peacefully in the stern of the boat while they were
frantically trying to keep their little boat afloat. When they
try to wake him up, they speak to him in a compressed,
terse lament: "Teacher, don't you care if we drown?" A
brief invocation, laying claim to their relationship with
their rabbi—and then a sharp, pointed complaint. Jesus
wakes and calms the wind and the waves (Mark 4:35–41).
Jesus steps into the divine role not only in his power over
creation (Ps 107:28–29), but also when he hears their cries
for help and responds to save.

Jesus *is* God's answer to Israel's laments: God has torn
open the heavens and come down to be with people, to
dwell among them, to be one of them. In the Gospels, Jesus

appears on both sides of the lament—he laments, and he hears. He weeps, and he dries the tears.

WEAK ENOUGH TO HEAR, STRONG ENOUGH TO SAVE

In one of my favorite songs, Nichole Nordeman sings, "O great God, be small enough to hear me now."[9] Not big enough. Small enough. That's how the book of Hebrews describes Jesus, as a "small enough" God, the mighty One of the universe reduced to a frail, dying, weeping body.

The letter to the Hebrews is in many ways a mystery. For one thing, it doesn't seem to be a letter; it looks more like a treatise or a sermon. Nobody knows who wrote it, or when, or where. Whoever wrote it gave us a gift, because it gives us an image for Jesus that doesn't occur anywhere else in Scripture.

The four Gospels describe Jesus' earthly life. Hebrews gives us a glimpse into Jesus' heavenly life—his risen life after the resurrection. In Hebrews, Jesus is the great high priest who knew in his own flesh and bones the same fears and griefs that we struggle with, and who waits to receive our cries for help with mercy. The one who lamented now hears prayers of lament.

> Therefore, since we have a great high priest who has ascended into heaven, Jesus the Son of God, let us hold firmly to the faith we profess. For we do not have a high priest who is unable to empathize with our weaknesses, but we have one who has been tempted in every way, just as we are—yet he did not sin. Let us then approach God's throne of grace with confidence, so that

9. Nichole Nordeman, "Small Enough," track 5 on *This Mystery*, Sparrow Records, 2000.

we may receive mercy and find grace to help us
in our time of need. (Heb 4:14–16)

For the author of Hebrews, what qualifies Jesus to be
"the great high priest," the one who hears cries for help
in heaven and responds with mercy? Is it his holiness,
his power, his divine nature? No. It's his humanity. *Being
human* is what qualifies him. Even more so, it's being a
human who suffered and died. It's Jesus' flesh and blood
and bones—torn flesh, spilled blood, bruised bones—that
make him fit to be the heavenly high priest (Heb 2:14). Jesus can "free those who all their lives were held in slavery
by their fear of death" (Heb 2:15) because he himself tasted
that fear and knew that death. You need not fear death,
writes the author of Hebrews, because the pioneer of your
salvation forged a path through death and into the eternal
Sabbath rest (Heb 2:9–10).

There's more: Jesus' flesh-and-blood existence doesn't
stop with his earthly life. It continues in the heavenly realm.
The Gospels insist that Jesus rose again *in his body*—the same
body with which he lived. His hands and feet still had the
scars from the nails to prove it; his side still had a wound in it
from the Roman soldier's sword (Luke 24:39–40; John 20:20,
27). That's the point of the empty tomb. Jesus' soul didn't as-
cend into heaven; his body did. To be sure, it's a transformed
body. The Gospel writers struggle to make sense of it. People
don't always recognize Jesus right away in his transformed,
resurrected body. He appears and disappears and walks
through walls. Still, it's a body. He even eats fish to prove he's
not a ghost (Luke 24:42–43; John 21:9–13).

So when Jesus ascends into heaven, he brings his
resurrected body with him. This is an astonishing truth,
one that stretches the imagination to the breaking point.
How can (transformed) human flesh and blood dwell in
the heavenly realm, the domain of souls and angels and

35

the invisible God? Somehow, it does. In Hebrews, the risen Jesus carries the sacrifice of his own blood right into the heavenly throne room with him (Heb 9:11–12; 10:19–20). It's easy to read this as a metaphor. But the Gospel accounts insist that it's not.

With that final act, Jesus ends sacrifices once and for all (Heb 10:10–14). The only sacrifices needed now are those of prayers: both praises and laments. Jesus' wounded (and healed, and transformed) body sits on the throne of heaven, and it's to that wounded body that people now lament. And he waits eagerly to hear those laments, ready with his mercy. Like God, it's lament he longs to hear.

REFLECTION

1. Why does it matter that Jesus lamented?

2. Why does God invite people to "stand in the breach" between people and God's judgment?

3. What's the significance of Jesus' risen body in the heavenly realm? How might this reframe our understanding of what heaven is?

3

YOUR KINGDOM COME

"... the whole creation has been groaning ..."
(Rom 8:22)

"... your kingdom come." (Matt 6:10; Luke 11:2)

IS DOUBT A SIN?

THE FIRST TIME I encountered the view that doubt is a sin,
I was startled. I was lucky to be raised in a church and men-
tored by pastors who invited me to ask questions, even hard
questions, as I matured and grew into faith. I was also raised
by a physicist—so wondering about things and asking questions was enthusiastically endorsed in my household.

Unwavering faith comes easily to some people. Not to
me. For me faith has often been "a leap into the darkness
of the unknown, a flight into empty air," which is how the
theologian Karl Barth describes it. Barth goes on to say,
"For all faith is both simple and difficult; for all alike it is

a scandal, a hazard, a 'Nevertheless'; to all it presents the same embarrassment and the same promise; for all it is a leap into the void. And it is possible for all, only because for all it is equally impossible."[1]

Lament, of course, also contains a "Nevertheless"—a "but," a "yet"—when it makes the turn toward stubborn trust even in the midst of suffering and sorrow. "But, I will trust in you." "Yet, I will sing of your steadfast love." Lament is praise from within the whirlwind, not in the stillness after the storm. It seems to me that's why lament, even at its most bitter, still represents an act of faith. Even when it can't even manage that turn to praise, even if the "yet" dies on the lips of the lamenter, it's still an act of faith, because it turns toward God to address God.

Lamenting is not a sin. It doesn't display a lack of faith or trust. It reveals the opposite: a deep and abiding trust, however faint, however shaken, however wounded, in a God who hears the cries of God's children.

Is doubt, then, a sin? Of course not. We cannot will ourselves into confidence any more than we can will ourselves out of depression or into a good mood. That's true about mental illnesses, over which we have little control, but it's also about the way that we sometimes seem to be at the mercy of our emotions more generally.

Emotions and Faith

I often ask my ethics students if they're morally responsible for their emotions. Many say no. And they're right—but only partly. Others say yes—and they are also right, but again only partly. The question of whether we can be held to account for emotions (like doubt, or anger, or fear, or hatred) is an old one. One of the most thoughtful answers

1. Barth, *Epistle to the Romans*, 98, 99.

comes from a man named Thomas, who wrote a treatise on the emotions (or the "passions") about 750 years ago.[2] Thomas was from a city in Italy called Aquino, so he became known as Thomas Aquinas.

Thomas proposed that we're not initially morally responsible for our emotions, because they're simply spontaneous reactions. They are "bodily judgments of the situation at hand."[3] Modern scientists might say something similar about our bodies. Our bodies sense a threat, and they react: our hearts race, our palms sweat. But, at the same time, Thomas thought, our emotional responses are shaped by our reason and our will; they arise from things we believe about the world around us. We *are* morally responsible for the ways we shape our emotions, Thomas suggested, when we exercise our reason and our will, when we choose to nurture or sustain or feed those emotions.

For example, think of the expression "nurse a grudge." Another example is what happens if you find that you're attracted to the wrong person—say, to someone who's married to someone else, or to your roommate's significant other. That initial attraction might be spontaneous. "That's just how I feel!" you might say. But as soon as you start allowing yourself to daydream about that person, or deliberately try to spend as much time as possible with them, you've taken hold of that emotion and made it yours; you've become responsible for it.

Another possibility is that a false belief sparked the emotion. The best example of this is probably racist fears or racist judgments. If one believes that one's race is superior to another race, or that all members of a certain race are inherently dangerous or untrustworthy, this false belief might give rise to fear or even hatred of that other racial

2. Thomas Aquinas, *Summa Theologica*, I–II, q.24, 34, 39.

3. Mattison, *Introducing Moral Theology*, 81.

group. For Thomas, that means that we can be held morally responsible for that negative reaction even if it's spontaneous, because it's grounded in a failure of truth—a failure to see the world rightly. If there's no possible way we could have known the truth, then that lets us off the hook, at least temporarily. But if we have the resources available to know the truth, we are responsible for a false belief.

What does all this have to do with doubt? I think it means that we should be gentle toward people who struggle with doubt. One way to respond to the gut reaction of doubt is with lament. Rather than ignore doubt, or pretend it's not there, or feel guilty about it, one can shape one's doubt—take responsibility for it, as it were—by naming it and even daring to complain about it, perhaps to grieve over it. Lament is a cry for all those who suffer, including the doubters, including those who feel the sharp sting of fear that what they believe might not be true, or who feel the ache of loss for what they once had.

Like all activities, lament shapes the person who laments. It inclines them in a certain direction. Lament inclines toward hope. It leans toward the light while still in the darkness. It takes doubts and fears over God's silence and shapes them into prayer. Lament insists that God does not disdain or turn aside these challenges but receives them as offerings. Even doubt. Even despair. Even the cry "My God, why have you forsaken me?"

PATIENT ENDURANCE AND GOD'S WILL

Still, the New Testament doesn't always seem to endorse lament or complaint. One of the main Christian virtues praised in the New Testament is patient endurance, which is the Greek word *hypomonē* (sometimes translated patience, perseverance, or endurance). In Jesus' parable of the sower, the seed that falls on good soil and produces a crop is a metaphor for the people who receive God's word and "bear fruit with patient endurance [*hypomonē*]" (Luke 8:15).

Sometime around the year AD 57, the apostle Paul wrote to the Christians in Rome, "we also boast in our sufferings, knowing that suffering produces [patient] endurance, and [patient] endurance produces character, and character produces hope" (Rom 5:3 NRSV). In another letter, he instructs his fellow Christians to patiently endure their sufferings (2 Cor 1:6). In two different letters, he writes, "Rejoice *always*!" (Phil 4:4; 1 Thess 5:16, emphasis added).

The first thing to observe is that many of the Christians who received these letters were suffering. Nobody needs to be told to endure if things are going great. For that matter, nobody needs to be instructed to "Rejoice!" if they're already feeling joyful. A few years before Paul wrote his letter, in AD 49, the Roman emperor Claudius had expelled Jews from Rome because of disturbances provoked by someone named Chrestus—probably a mixup with the name Christos, or Christ.[4] Surely many Jews who worshiped Jesus were caught up in this expulsion, since the Romans would not have distinguished between Jews who worshiped Jesus and Jews who did not. Paul's letter was written under the early days of Nero's reign, several years before the great fire of Rome that prompted Nero to blame—and execute—many Christians for the fire's devastation. Still, Christians in Rome (whether Jews or gentiles) faced some suspicion and hostility in the early 50s.

The second thing to say is that the same Paul also wrote, "Mourn with those who mourn." Yes, "rejoice with those who rejoice," but also, "mourn with those who mourn" (Rom 12:15). Paul knew that people mourn. He never told

4. Wright and Bird, *New Testament in its World*, 355.

them to stop. Instead, he said that the church is like a body; if one part is in pain, the whole thing is in pain. If one part is weeping, the whole is weeping (1 Cor 12:26). Paul himself mourns. He lays bare the anguish of his own soul in Rom 9, as he wrestles with the pain of why more of his fellow Jews haven't turned to Christ as their Messiah.

A couple decades after Jesus' death and resurrection, Christians in the city of Thessalonika (in modern-day Turkey) began to worry about Christians who had died: what would happen to them when Christ returned? Paul writes to instruct them on the resurrection of the dead "so that you may not grieve as others do who have no hope" (1 Thess 4:13). He does not write, "so that you may not grieve." There's no comma after the word "grieve" in those instructions. He writes, essentially, "so that you might grieve with hope." Even belief in the resurrection doesn't exempt people from grief when their loved ones die. Even Jesus—who held the power of life and death in his hands— even Jesus wept at the grave of a friend.

Jesus also gives instructions about patient endurance. He tells his followers to persevere in prayer and never give up. The kind of perseverance and endurance that he recommends is the persistence of a friend who comes to knock on your door in the middle of the night because he needs to borrow something even though it's midnight. And he knocks and knocks and pounds on the door until you finally get exasperated and get out of bed and give him what he wants (Luke 11:5–10).

The kind of patience that Jesus recommends is that of the stubborn widow who pesters an unjust judge over and over again with her relentless petitions until the judge finally caves in and gives her justice (Luke 18:1–8). Pray like *that*, Jesus tells his followers. God isn't like a sleeping friend or an unjust judge; God doesn't mind being pestered in prayer. In fact, God seems to like it.

To be sure, there are limits placed around this practice of pestering in prayer. One Jewish tradition calls this kind of prayer "boldness with regard to heaven" (*chutzpa k'lapei shamaya*). One can see this boldness when God tells Moses that God has had enough of "your people" and Moses retorts that Israel is "*your* people"—not Moses' people but *God's* people, now and forever, because that's what God promised (Exod 32:7, 11). One sees it highlighted in the way that later rabbis reflected on the boldness of Moses, Abraham, and Job in their writings on the biblical texts.

Yet as Belden Lane writes, it's "a boldness tempered by limits." One of the limits is "the framework" of the covenant that God made with Israel. God and Israel are bound together by steadfast love, by the promises that each has made to the other. Likewise the lament pattern provides certain boundaries, since it offers a formal structure for wrestling with God in prayer (invocation, complaint, petition, trust). The invocation itself is designed to call upon a relationship with God, no matter how strained or distant that relationship might be. The ultimate goal of "boldness with regard to heaven" is not to insult God or to try to pull a lever and force God to act. Instead, its goal is "intimacy with God."[5]

Suffering

So patient endurance can involve crying out repeatedly in prayer to God and asking for help, which is the heart of lament—crying out in the midst of suffering. Yet the

5. Lane concludes, "Only as it engaged the believer in the most intense and loving contest with God could the presumption be approved" (Lane, "Hutzpa K'lapei Shamaya," 581). Lane writes that the final limit is "the awareness that such verbal extremity is permitted only in extreme emergencies" (579).

meaning and value of suffering raises another potential obstacle to the complaint element of the lament. If God directs and governs all things, then does not suffering fall into God's domain? Some Christian traditions have even proposed that God causes suffering for our education, or our discipline, or for our own good. (Other religious and philosophical traditions have sometimes agreed; one slogan of Stoic philosophers was "to suffer is to learn.") If God directs and governs even our suffering, then what gives us the right to complain about it?

As the Christian philosopher Nicholas Wolterstorff asks in the title of one of his essays, "If God is good and sovereign, why lament?"[6] The Reformed tradition (the branch of Protestant Christianity originating from John Calvin) places special emphasis on the sovereignty of God, which is the belief that God has control over everything in the universe and directs all things to God's purposes.

Calvin's understanding of God's sovereignty led him to believe that God sends us suffering in order to reform and mold us, to call us to repentance, to teach us humility, and to draw us closer to God.[7] Wolterstorff himself hails from the Reformed tradition. In his essay, he explains Calvin's view, and he acknowledges "the massive weights of our [Reformed] theological tradition." But, he says, he chooses to follow the example of the psalmist. "In so doing," he writes, "I have on my side the biblical examples" of lament.[8]

Like Wolterstorff, I don't believe that God *causes* suffering. Ever. I know that Christians of good faith may disagree with me on this matter. They point to verses in Scripture that describe suffering as a form of fatherly

6. Wolterstorff, "If God is Good," 42–52. See also Charry, "May We Trust," 95–108.

7. Wolterstorff, "If God is Good," 48–49.

8. Wolterstorff, "If God is Good," 50.

discipline, as in the book of Hebrews: "Endure hardship as discipline; God is treating you as his children. . . . God disciplines us for our good" (Heb 12:7, 10). Can God use hardship for our good? No doubt. God uses everything for our good and not for our harm. But does God smite us with cancer or coronavirus or unemployment in order to teach us a lesson? Surely not. I cannot square this picture of God with everything else I believe to be true about the God revealed in Scripture—a God who promises rest to the weary and shelter to the bruised (Matt 11:28–30), a God who is near to the brokenhearted (Ps 34:18).

When the author of the letter to the Hebrews tells his readers to endure hardship as if it were a form of discipline, he's writing to a congregation that is struggling (and sometimes failing) to remain faithful to Jesus in the face of numerous pressures. The author reminds them that they "endured a hard struggle with sufferings" (Heb 10:32). Some of them were "publicly exposed to abuse and persecution" (Heb 10:33). Some of them were in prison; some of them had their possessions taken away (Heb 10:34). All this suggests a context of intense social pressure and even persecution because of their identity as Christians. Since we don't know where or when the letter was written, we don't know exactly what kind of persecution it was, but it fits with what we know of the situation of some first-century Christians in the Roman Empire.

Over and over, the author encourages them not to give up and warns them about the dire consequences of abandoning their faith. He holds up Jesus' endurance in the face of hostility and suffering as a model for them, "so that you may not grow weary or lose heart" (Heb 12:3). He reminds them that, unlike Jesus, they "have not yet resisted to the point of shedding your blood" (Heb 12:4). In all these ways, the author renarrates their suffering: it is a sign not of God's indifference or nonexistence but a sign, paradoxically, of God's love for them. They suffer persecution because they bear the name of Jesus.

Likewise, the apostle Peter told the recipients of his first letter to rejoice in their trials, because their trials "have come so that the proven genuineness of your faith . . . may result in praise, glory and honor when Jesus Christ is revealed" (1 Pet 1:7). Peter, like the author of Hebrews, has in mind a particular kind of suffering; the trials the early Christians were undergoing were the trials of being persecuted for following Christ.

All that to say, the advice about suffering in Scripture is often about a certain kind of suffering—facing persecution because of loyalty to Jesus—and not directly about the kinds of suffering we face simply by being human. Christians haven't always even agreed about the meaning of persecution as a form of suffering. Some Christians wondered if God caused persecution in order to test and strengthen the church, while others have thought that persecution was a tool of the devil, designed to harm and harass God's people.

What I see in Scripture and in my own experience is a God who comes alongside us in our suffering. What I see in Scripture and in my own life is that God can work good out of evil. In the first book of the Bible, when a man named Joseph comes to face-to-face again, years later, with the brothers who deliberately sold him into slavery and then lied to their father about it, Joseph tells them, "You intended to harm me, but God intended it for good" (Gen 50:20), or, in the elegant old words of the King James, "But as for you, ye thought evil against me; but God meant it unto good" (Gen 50:20 KJV).

Do we sometimes grow stronger or deeper or more mature through our suffering? Yes. God works all things for good. Are we sometimes driven to repentance or compassion because of suffering? Yes. God works all things for good. God doesn't make us suffer but God can redeem it when we do.

When pastor Glen Wiberg lost his son Carl to multiple sclerosis at the age of twenty-seven, he preached a sermon about a woman who broke an alabaster jar of costly perfume and poured it on Jesus' head (in ancient times, a gesture of honor). The people who witnessed this event were indignant. Even the disciples complained about the waste of such valuable perfume, objecting that it should have been sold and the money given to the poor. But Jesus rebukes them, saying, "She has done a beautiful thing for me." He renarrates her action as an act of preparation for his burial (since dead bodies were anointed before their burial) (Mark 14:3–6). Wiberg says of this episode,

> One of the most difficult facets of suffering in many forms lies in the ancient question "why" asked by the disciples in protest to the breaking of the costly alabaster box and precious ointment. And asked if suffering like Carl's and watching the slow deterioration of body and mind in one so bright and young we have to ask "Why this waste?" . . .
>
> The good news I want to share with you is Nothing is Wasted, neither the precious ointment, nor the alabaster jar, nor its brokenness. For when all is said and done everything in the long run depends on God's doing, where everything finally serves his purpose, gathering up the fragments in resurrection so that nothing goes down the drain, nothing at all is lost. It will be proclaimed in his remembrance, and to his glory. Amen.[9]

9. Wiberg, quoted in "'Pietism is the Way.'"

When Nicholas Wolterstorff lost his twenty-five-year-old son Eric to a climbing accident, he wrote that he couldn't find any answer that explained why his son had died. He rejects the appalling idea that God deliberately shook the mountain to make his son fall, but he also rejects the conclusion that God was simply powerless to stop it. "I cannot fit it all together by saying, '[God] did it,' but neither can I do so by saying, 'There was nothing [God] could do about it.' . . . I can only, with Job, endure. . . . I have no explanation. I can do nothing else than endure in the face of this deepest and most painful of mysteries. I believe in God the Father Almighty, maker of heaven and earth and resurrecter of Jesus Christ. I also believe that my son's life was cut off in its prime."[10]

This is the endurance of lament. "I can only endure." It shows us that patient endurance doesn't mean the rejection of lament. It might mean its embrace. Sometimes, the only way we can endure is through lament.

SOMEDAY: A LAMENT FOR THE IN-BETWEEN TIMES

While I was sheltering in place in the spring and summer of 2020, I thought a lot about the word "Someday." One day I was listening to one of my favorite podcasts (*Make Me Smart*). Like so many other people, the hosts were working from home. At the very end of the show, just before signing off, one of the hosts mentioned how much they missed being able to see their producers through the glass in the studio where they usually worked, and the other host whispered, just before signing off, "Someday."

With one word, I was undone. *Someday.*

10. Wolterstorff, *Lament for a Son*, 67–68.

The Christian way of thinking about reality is that we're essentially living in-between two worlds, or two ages. The first world, or the first age, has begun to pass away, but we're still living in its grip. The second world, or the new age, has begun to arrive but is not yet fully here. This tension is sometimes called "the now and the not yet." The "now" is all the ways God has already accomplished salvation and freed us from sin and fear; the "not yet" are the things that remain to happen for God's justice and peace to fully triumph. The not yet is the "someday."

The first age, or the old age, is life as we know it—our daily lives as citizens of various countries and members of certain families, the world where we work and vote and love and fight and mourn. In the old age, injustice and violence often rule the day. The strong win; the weak are trampled. One Gospel writer vividly described the devil as the prince of this age (John 12:31; 14:30; 16:11).

The next age, the new age, is the reign of God, or the kingdom (the domain) of God. Justice will rule the day. Hierarchies will be overturned: the strong laid low, the weak exalted; the hungry filled. (That's why it's sometimes called "the upside-down kingdom.") The lion will lay down with the lamb and all creation will dwell in perfect harmony and peace and wholeness. Justo González calls this *Mañana*, the tomorrow toward which we journey and for which we long. My mentor Allen Verhey called it "God's good future."[11]

In the Christian imagination, Jesus' death and resurrection inaugurated the new age. Jesus' death shattered death. On the day called Pentecost, the outpouring of the Holy Spirit on women and men, on the poor and the wealthy, signaled the arrival of God's new day (Acts 2:1–4, 16–18).

11. González, *Mañana*, 157–67; Verhey, *Christian Art of Dying*, 202–3, 263–64, 268.

And yet: people still die. The strong and arrogant still win; the weak are still often trampled. Sin still rages. The prince of this world still seems to rule. *Why?* asks lament. *How long?* asks lament.

In the Christian imagination, the inauguration of the new age is like the dawn. The dawn is not the sunrise; it's the sign that the sunrise is on its way. The sun is still below the horizon but its light has already begun to lighten the darkness of the night. It sends slivers of silver and pink and orange as messengers to herald its arrival.

Just as the dawn signals the sure coming of the sun, churches—local congregations or gatherings of Christians all around the world—are supposed to be the dawn. They are meant to be the heralds and signals of the surely coming reign of God, where the weak are lifted up and the hungry are filled and people are reconciled across the boundaries of class and race, the place where we get to see glimpses of what that coming kingdom looks like—an unimaginably beautiful and capacious space where all the nations gather and are healed and share their gifts (Rev 7:9; 21:24; 22:2).

Churches have not always lived up to this calling. They've often failed in humiliating and shocking ways. They've exploited the vulnerable instead of sheltering them. They've grasped power instead of giving themselves away in love. They've pledged allegiance to one nation-state instead of behaving as citizens of a kingdom that transcends national boundaries. Other communities have often been much better at imaging the coming kingdom of God than churches have, reminding Christians that God's Spirit is not confined to the church.

This failure is one more thing to add to the list of complaints to be made into laments. It's one more reason that churches desperately need to adopt lament as one of their primary languages of prayer—not only to lament the hurts of the world but to lament the ways they've sometimes contributed to that hurt, for the ways they've fallen short of their calling to mirror God's beautiful domain. Of course, some churches already have lament written into their DNA, whether it's because they're an underground church dodging state persecution in China, or a mobile church of Syrian Christians on the move fleeing war, or an African-American church bearing the burden of slavery's legacy and the sting of racism's ongoing wear and tear.

Lament is for the wide and often painful gap between the dawn and the sunrise. It's for the agonizingly long pause that has gone on for thousands of years now between the first glimpse of dawn and the sunrise still to come. It's for life in-between the times: in-between Christ's first coming and his second one, in-between the old age and the new one to come.

Christians all over the world pray "Your kingdom come" as part of the prayer that Jesus taught his followers to pray. It rings out day and night before God's throne. "Your kingdom come" is a petition. It's like Isaiah's heartfelt cry, "Oh, that you would rend the heavens and come down . . . !" (Isa 64:1). *Come down!* It's also like the plea at the very end of the book of Revelation, one of the last words in all of Scripture: "Come, Lord Jesus!" (Rev 22:20). Please come. It's a petition prayed in the context of all the ways that God's kingdom has not yet come, for the ways that God's justice and peace and harmony do not yet reign. It's a petition for all the times we whisper, *Someday*.

Paradoxically, Jesus declares that those who mourn or weep are the blessed ones, the happy ones, the flourishing ones. "Blessed are those who mourn, for they will be comforted" (Matt 5:4). "Blessed are you who weep now, for you will laugh" (Luke 6:21b).[12] How can this be? Perhaps they're

12. For more on this beatitude see Eklund, *Beatitudes through*

declared blessed because they're the ones who will be comforted. (Jesus also says, "Woe to you who laugh now, for you will mourn and weep," Luke 6:25b.) Wolterstorff ponders another reason why Jesus might have declared a blessing on those who mourn.

> Who then are the mourners? The mourners are those who have caught a glimpse of God's new day, who ache with all their being for that day's coming, and who break out into tears when confronted with its absence. . . . They are the ones who realize that in God's realm there is no one who suffers oppression and who ache whenever they see someone beat down. . . . They are the ones who realize that in God's realm of peace there is neither death nor tears and who ache whenever they see someone crying tears over death.[13]

All Creation Groans

According to Paul, all of creation waits along with humankind for God's "not yet." He writes to Christians in Rome in the first century,

> For the creation waits in eager expectation for the children of God to be revealed. . . . [T]he creation itself will be liberated from its bondage to decay and brought into the freedom and glory of the children of God. We know that the whole creation has been groaning as in the pains of childbirth right up to the present time. Not only so, but we ourselves, who have the firstfruits of the Spirit, groan inwardly as we wait eagerly for

---

the Ages, 98–121.

13. Wolterstorff, *Lament for a Son*, 85–86.

> our adoption to sonship, the redemption of our
> bodies. (Rom 8:19–23)

The whole universe strains toward that Someday. Stars and trees and streams anticipate with longing the day of God's reign. How can that be? In the book of Isaiah, the mountains and hills burst into song, and the trees of the field clap their hands with joy, at the sight of God's redemption of the people of Israel (Isa 55:12). In the Psalms, the skies declare the glory of God (Ps 19:1). Jesus tells the religious leaders that if his disciples stopped shouting praises to God, the rocks would cry out in their place (Luke 19:39–40).

I grew up in the company of a writer who captured this brilliantly in her children's books. Madeleine L'Engle wrote about stars who sing and who take on human shape to join forces with children battling mysterious dark powers. (She has good biblical support, since in the ancient Jewish and Christian imaginations, stars were angels.)[14] In one of her books, even mitochondria dance with joy; even these microscopic organic inhabitants of our cells can be swayed toward the darkness and can be redeemed and set free to praise again.[15]

It's easy to forget that human beings are not separate from "nature" or from the rest of creation but are in fact part of it. This is true in biology and in Scripture. When God makes human beings, he makes them from the dirt. In the original Hebrew, it's impossible to miss this because it's a pun using the name of Adam. In Hebrew, the word *adam* can mean "a man," "humanity," or the proper name "Adam." (It's like naming someone Human.) In Hebrew, the word for dirt or dust is *adamah*. So when Genesis says, "Then the LORD God formed a man from the ground," it's saying,

14. Allison, "Magi's Angel," 17–41.

15. L'Engle, *Wrinkle in Time* and *Wind in the Door*.

"God formed *adam* from the *adamah*" (Gen 2:7). If you've ever been to a funeral and heard the words, "dust to dust, ashes to ashes," that's the same principle. From dust we were taken; to dust we shall return.

All creatures, all created things, are subject to decay and death. Human beings go from dust to dust. Trees age and die. Even stars die. It's a natural part of the cycle of life. But Paul, in his letter to the Romans, makes the audacious claim that creation "will be liberated from its bondage to decay" (Rom 8:21). As Paul tells it, decay is not the natural way of things but is a form of bondage. The creation has been "subjected to frustration," he claims (Rom 8:20).

The word frustration can also mean futility, "in the sense of the futility of an object which does not function as it was designed to do . . . or, more precisely, which has been given a role for which it was not designed and which is unreal or illusory."[16] In the first two chapters of Genesis, God repeatedly describes the world God created as "good." The land and the seas: good. Tomato plants and peach trees and grapevines: good. Stars and the moon and the sun: good. Whales and white-throated sparrows, leopards and marmots: good. After God creates humanity, it is all together declared to be *very* good.

The Hebrew word for good is *tov*—a word that can also mean harmonious, beautiful, or fitting. In God's good creation, everything is in place; the people and the animals and the land dwell together in harmony and peace. And everything has its role: people are designated the caretakers, who are assigned to watch over, protect, and govern the rest of the created world. The plants are given to both people and the other animals for food.

But for the apostle Paul, the efforts of both humans and the created world have become frustrated, or futile. For

16. Dunn, *Romans 1–8*, 470.

New Testament scholar James Dunn, humanity's futility (de-scribed in Rom 1:18) is the failure to see ourselves as crea-tures (created beings) rather than as creators, as dependent rather than independent, as stewards rather than lords.

Creation's futility occurs when the earth and its good inhabitants (trees, animals, birds) are not understood as "God's creation to be ordered by God."[17] Creation's purpose is frustrated when people use and abuse the creation for their own gains. As Dunn writes, "creation was not party to Adam's failure but was drawn into it nonetheless."[18]

Why, then, does Paul say that the creation "was subjected to frustration . . . by the will of the one who subjected it" (Rom 8:20)? Why would it be God's will to subject the creation to futility? Dunn suggests that Paul has compressed a complex sequence of thought into an abbreviated form: "God subjected all things to Adam, and that included subjecting creation to fallen Adam, to share in his fallenness," but this is "not an end of God's dealings but a stage in his purpose, the means by which the self-destructiveness of sin can be drawn out and destroyed, and creation restored to its proper function as the envi-ronment for God's restored children."[19]

The end goal, as Paul goes on to say in the next verse, is that "the creation itself will be liberated from its bond-age to decay and brought into the freedom and glory of the children of God" (Rom 8:21). When we humans long for freedom and glory, when we long for that *Mañana*, the rest of creation longs for it, too.

The futility of creation—its participation in the "fall" resulting from humanity's disobedience and rebellion—is related to what philosophers sometimes call "natural evils":

17. Dunn, *Romans 1–8*, 470.

18. Dunn, *Romans 1–8*, 470.

19. Dunn, *Romans 1–8*, 471.

earthquakes and tsunamis and viruses, cancer and torna-
does and deadly allergies. Natural evils are typically distinguished from what philosophers call "moral evils," which
include all the harmful and hateful things we human beings do to ourselves and to others. To identify these natural
things as evil (and not just the way nature happens to be) is
to claim that they're not part of God's purposes, not part of
God's good plan for the created world—or at least that their
power to harm falls outside God's good purposes.

This makes sense if we think about how much havoc
the natural world can wreak on us. 230,000 people died when
a tsunami hit southeast India in 2004. It's estimated that 40
percent of the dead were children. I still remember weeping
as I saw, on the evening news, children's bodies washing up
on the shore. And as I write this, the novel coronavirus has
already killed hundreds of thousands of people around the
globe.

Paul (and the whole of Scripture) insists that the
creation itself is not evil. How could it be? It was made by
God and everything God made is good—the snow and the
sand and the wind, all of it (Gen 1:3, 10, 12, 18, 21, 25, 31).
But the creation, like humanity, is damaged and broken
and frustrated from its intended harmony. And it groans
under that burden, longing to be set free (Rom 8:22), just
as human beings groan while eagerly waiting the redemption of their bodies (Rom 8:23). Note that humans eagerly
await not only the saving of their souls but the redemption
of their *bodies*.

Paul has in view here not only (or perhaps not at all)
the hope of heaven, but the greater hope of a new creation,
of the creation itself remade and set free. This is the vision
at the end of Revelation, when a reborn city of Jerusalem
descends from the heavenly realm into the earthly one,
when God creates a new heaven and new earth of perfect

harmony, complete with rivers and trees (Rev 21–22). In another letter, Paul writes a whole chapter about his firm belief that the entire Christian system depends on hope in the resurrection of the *body*, and explores what that resurrected body might be like (1 Cor 15). In his next letter to the same Christians in the ancient city of Corinth, he writes that they "groan" as they wait in longing to be "clothed" with their resurrected bodies, which he describes as "our heavenly dwelling" (2 Cor 5:2–4).

The word "groaning" is a lament word.[20] When Abraham's descendants were taken into slavery in Egypt, they groaned as they suffered, and God heard their cries (Exod 2:23–25). In the Psalms, lamenters sometimes groan as they cry out to God with their tears, complaints, and petitions (Pss 6:6; 31:10; 38:9; 102:5). Jerusalem and all her inhabitants groaned as they suffered the anguish of siege, defeat, and exile (Lam 1:4, 8, 11, 21, 22).

When Paul says that the creation is groaning as if "in the pains of childbirth," he's using a pretty common metaphor for the onset of the ending of this old age and the arrival of the next age. Some other Jewish thinkers around this time used this image. Jesus used it to talk about the painful turmoil that would accompany the end of the old age (Mark 13:8).

As a metaphor, it's a lot like the dawn. It's a signal that something else is about to arrive.

REFLECTION

1. In Christian thought, what is the "now" and what is "the not yet"?

---

20. For a detailed study of the word "groaning" (*stenazō*) and related words in the New Testament, see Öhler, "To Mourn, Weep, Lament and Groan," 154–64.

2. Justo González writes that God's *mañana* is not only hope for tomorrow, it is also a judgment on today. Why would this be?

3. If all of creation longs for redemption, what does that say about humanity's relationship to nature?

4

PENITENCE AND PROTEST

"Have mercy on me, O God . . .
Against you, you only, have I sinned . . ." (Ps 51:1a, 4a)

"If I have sinned, what have I done to you,
    you who see everything we do?
Why have you made me your target?
    Have I become a burden to you?" (Job 7:20)

LAMENT HAS TWO MAIN streams: protest and penitence. This is a little oversimplified. The two streams often cross and mingle with one another. Some laments don't fit neatly into one category or the other. Sometimes a cry for help is just a cry for help, not a protest or a plea for forgiveness. But for the sake of clarity, I'll distinguish these two streams so that I can explore their contours with you.

PENITENCE

The first main stream is penitence, or repentance. Some-times the cause of the distress or sorrow that gives rise to lament is sin—our failures, our mistakes, our willfulness, our rebellion against the good. We fall short in so many ways, and we wound ourselves and others. Some of the la-ments in the Hebrew Bible are confessions of sin, expres-sions of repentance, and pleas for God's mercy. One of the most well-known is Ps 51, which explains its setting in a liner note that precedes the psalm.

David was the second king of Israel and its most be-loved king. He's described once as "a man after [God's] own heart" (1 Sam 13:14). But David's passionate nature also got him into trouble. When a beautiful married woman named Bathsheba catches his eye, he has her brought to the palace, rapes her, and sends her home. When Bathsheba sends word that she's pregnant, David tries to coax her husband home from the field of battle to sleep with her, but her husband, a man of honor, refuses the king's disingenuous offer; he will not indulge in luxuries while his men are sleeping out in the fields. To cover up his crime, David has her husband killed and takes Bathsheba as his wife.

God sends the prophet Nathan to confront David. Na-than tricks David into feeling outrage toward his own behav-ior by disguising David's action in a parable about a rich man who forcibly takes a beloved lamb away from a poor man (2 Sam 12:1–12). David is forced to see what he has done. He confesses to Nathan, "I have sinned against the LORD" (2 Sam 12:13). In an act of mercy, God spares David's life. But there is also judgment for David's sins: "because by doing this you have shown utter contempt for the LORD, the son born to you will die" (2 Sam 12:14).

David then composes Ps 51, with its abundant peti-tions: "Have mercy on me . . . blot out my transgressions . . .

Wash away all my iniquity and cleanse me from my sin. . . . Cleanse me . . . wash me . . . Hide your face from my sins . . . Create in me a pure heart . . . Do not cast me from your presence . . . Deliver me from the guilt of bloodshed" (Ps 51:1, 2, 7, 9, 10, 11, 14). The "complaints" of David's lament are the anguished confession of his own sin:

> For I know my transgressions,
> and my sin is always before me.
> Against you, you only, have I sinned
>   and done what is evil in your sight;
> so you are right in your verdict
>   and justified when you judge. (Ps 51:3–4)

A hopeful if tentative turn toward praise is there, too, when David wonders if God will allow David to sing God's praise again:

> Open my lips, Lord,
>   and my mouth will declare your praise.
> My sacrifice, O God, is a broken spirit;
>   a broken and contrite heart
>   you, God, will not despise. (Ps 51:15, 17)

Some penitential laments are individual and deeply personal, like David's. Others are corporate or communal, as when the prophet Daniel put on sackcloth and covered himself with ashes (two visible signs of mourning) to confess Israel's sins and plead for God's forgiveness (Dan 9:1–19).

The penitential laments have played a prominent role in the Christian tradition. Psalm 51 eventually provided the lyrics for one of the most famous choral pieces ever sung: *Miserere mei Deus*, which is the Latin translation of the psalm's first line ("Have mercy on me, Lord"). It's sometimes known simply as the *Miserere* or the Allegri (after its composer, Gregorio Allegri, who set Ps 51 to music in the 1630s).

Sometime around the fifth or sixth century, Christians began designating seven psalms as "the penitential psalms": Ps 51, which we've already explored, as well as Pss 6, 32, 38, 102, 130, and 143. They're all psalms of lament, but many of them weave together strands of repentance and protest. Psalms 6 and 120 refer to God's anger (presumably toward sin or injustice) but don't include an explicit confession of sin or request for forgiveness. In Ps 38, David admits his guilt ("my sinful folly") but a few verses later cries out, "I seek only to do what is good" (Ps 38:5, 20). When the unnamed lamenter of Ps 130 sings, "Out of the depths I cry to you, LORD" (Ps 130:1), the "depths" could be the deep, dark places of sin or of suffering (see also Ps 69:14). Even in the psalms officially named as penitential, no neat or clear division exists between penitence and protest, between repentance and complaint.

So one important function of lament is to provide a space for repentance, for grief over one's own wrongdoing or the wrongdoing of others. It can make a space for individual repentance or for corporate confession. Lament is a powerful tool for naming our own sins as well as our participation in sinful and unjust structures. (See chapter 5 for examples.)

PROTEST

Other laments are protests. *Things are not as they should be.* As a protest, lament points to the painful gap between the way things should be and the way they are. As a prayer directed to God, it calls on God to account for the brokenness of the world, and it demands that God listen and respond—set right what is wrong, mend what is broken, bring light to the darkness—just as it is God's essential character to do so. God is a God of mercy: let there be mercy! God is a God of justice: let there be judgment on the violent and the oppressor! God's faithfulness to God's promises is at stake.

The book that records the words of the prophet Habakkuk begins with just this kind of lament. Habakkuk was likely active during one of the most traumatic episodes in Israel's history: the defeat of the southern kingdom of Judah at the hands of the Babylonian empire. The Judeans revolted against Babylon's rule in 598 BC. One year later, in 597 BC, many prominent Judeans, including the eighteen-year-old King Jehoiachin, were taken into exile. Ten years later, after a brutal siege of Jerusalem, the holy city was captured and the temple was destroyed. Habakkuk laments,

> How long, LORD, must I call for help,
>   but you do not listen?
> Or cry out to you, "Violence!"
>   but you do not save?
> Why do you make me look at injustice?
>   Why do you tolerate wrongdoing?
> Destruction and violence are before me;
>   there is strife, and conflict abounds.
> Therefore the law is paralyzed,
>   and justice never prevails.
> The wicked hem in the righteous,
>   so that justice is perverted. (Hab 1:2–4)

Habakkuk is pointing out the glaring gap between God's character and Israel's suffering. A God of justice seems to tolerate wrongdoing and injustice. A God of peace sees violence and does nothing. Unlike in the lament psalms, God responds directly to his prophet's complaints, promising that the end of their suffering "will certainly come" (Hab 2:3), and declaring judgment on the arrogant and unjust: "Woe to him who piles up stolen goods and makes himself wealthy by extortion! . . . Woe to him who builds his house by unjust gain. . . Woe to him who builds a city with bloodshed and establishes a town by injustice!" (Hab 2:6, 9, 12). In this way, God reassures Habakkuk that the LORD is not, as the prophet accuses, "silent when the wicked swallow up those more righteous than themselves" (Hab 1:13).

Yet the book does not end with redemption—only the promise and hope of it. So Habakkuk turns to the "yet" of the lament, stubbornly clinging to trust in God despite the suffering still raging all around him:

> Though the fig tree does not bud
>   and there are no grapes on the vines,
> though the olive crop fails
>   and the fields produce no food,
> though there are no sheep in the pen
>   and no cattle in the stalls,
> yet I will rejoice in the LORD,
>   I will be joyful in God my Savior. (Hab 3:17–18)

Besides the psalms and the prophets, there's another genre—a much more recent one—that also sounds the note of lament as a protest.

The Spirituals

If I could, I would pause here and play you a song. *Sometimes I feel like a motherless child, a long way from home.* Or, *Nobody knows the trouble I've seen.* Or, *Tell old Pharaoh to let my people go.* I currently worship in a multiracial church with a black pastor. Worship leaders are white and black and brown. We sing hymns, contemporary worship songs, and gospel songs. Every now and then the congregation or the choir sings a spiritual.

I've always enjoyed listening to spirituals, but for a long time I listened from a distance. There was a gap between my experience (comfortable, privileged) and the longing pain of the spirituals. Now they're starting to get a little deeper into my bones. I've lived in Uzbekistan and Baltimore City and, as a result, I've been more immersed in stories of suffering and oppression. I know I'll never feel them the way the descendants of slaves feel them. But I'm starting to learn how to weep with my African-American brothers and sisters. When a black person gets shot in Baltimore, that's my family, too.

James Cone speaks to this truth about the power of the spirituals when he writes, "To interpret the religious significance of [spirituals] for the black community, 'academic' tools are not enough. The interpreter must *feel* the Spirit; that is, one must feel one's way into the power of black music, responding both to its rhythm and the faith in experience it affirms."[1]

W. E. B. Du Bois called the spirituals the sorrow songs. In Du Bois's description, they were "the music of an unhappy people, of the children of disappointment; they tell of death and suffering and unvoiced longing toward a truer world, of misty wanderings and hidden ways."[2] But (like laments) they were also songs of hope: "Through all the sorrow of the Sorrow Songs there breathes a hope—a faith in the ultimate justice of things."[3]

Cone links the spirituals to the laments when he writes, "Their plaintive cry was the equivalent of Israel's prayer-complaint, 'How long, O Lord?'" Just as the laments invoke something true about God's character, so do the spirituals. In

1. Cone, *Spirituals and the Blues,* 4.

2. Du Bois, *Souls of Black Folk,* 183; quoted in Cone, *Spirituals and the Blues,* 13.

3. Du Bois, *Souls of Black Folk,* 189; quoted in Cone, *Spirituals and the Blues,* 13.

the midst of their suffering they affirmed the faithfulness of a God who liberates: "God is a God who frees slaves: Israelites in Egypt, Africans in the United States."[4] It's well-known that many of the spirituals were coded messages about escaping bondage. God is a God not only of spiritual freedom but of actual freedom—Israelites from exile in Babylon, Africans from slavery in the American South.

The spirituals don't accuse God of injustice or silence, as the protest laments sometimes do. Instead, the spirituals are a protest against the injustice of their situation, a protest whispered in solidarity and sung in metaphor, in defiance of their white masters, and in hope that the God who hears, hears *them*. Faith, as Du Bois wrote, in the ultimate justice of things.

Cone refers to the power of black music. Lament is sometimes viewed as a passive response, one of inaction instead of action; but laments (like the spirituals) are a form of power. They can knit a community together. They can strengthen weak knees and drooping hearts. When I first experienced worship in a black church, I wondered why there wasn't *more* lament; why so much praise, so much jubilation? Then one day a pastor said to me in passing: "you need a power that is greater than all the brokenness and losses." When the spirituals are joyful, their joy is a hard-won joy, one underwritten not by comfort but by hope in the midst of profound suffering. When they are sorrowful, they are nonetheless strong—in part because they see another day coming. In heaven, *all of God's children got shoes.*

Like other Christian laments, the spirituals also tap into the "now and not yet" dynamic that I discussed in chapter 3. God's salvation is "now" because sins are forgiven, because Jesus' death opened the gate to eternal life, because the Holy Ghost hovers over the world and speaks into hearts. But the

4. Cone, *Spirituals and the Blues,* 35.

"now" we live in is, also, so painful and so broken. When the slaves sang the spirituals, their "now" was almost unbearably awful. When we sing laments, it's because the "now" hurts so much. But it's also because there's something beyond our now; there's a *then*, a *not yet*, a *someday*. There's a future in which slaves are set free and the hungry are fed and the weeping are consoled.

Cone explains,

> To believe that there was hope in the midst of oppression meant that black slaves' vision of the future was not limited to their present state of slavery. . . . The present moment of slavery was thus transcended by faith in God's future, a liberated future. The divine future broke into their wretchedness. They seized God's future . . . as the strength for carving out a future for themselves. . . . To create the future in the "extreme situation" of American slavery was very difficult for black slaves. It meant accepting the burden and the risk of the "not yet."[5]

Embodied Lament-Protests

In this book, I'm mainly considering lament as it has been shaped by the traditions of Israel, by later Jewish traditions, and by Christian traditions. But lament is also a universal human cry. It arises from the common human experience of pain and suffering. Anthropologist Ruth Finnegan suggests that the lament or dirge is one of three traditional songs that occur in every human culture, along with the lullaby and the wedding song.[6] We all sing our little ones

5. Cone, *Spirituals and the Blues,* 87.

6. Lee, *Lyrics of Lament,* 7, 21–48.

to sleep; we all celebrate unions of love; we all grieve when our loved ones die.

Because lament is human (and not only Jewish or Christian), lamenting can be a form of solidarity with all who grieve or suffer. Lament can make us "deeply aware of a common vulnerability and anguish—a sense of shared *humanity*—that helps us place our suffering in a larger context and experience a new sense of connection with other suffering human beings amidst our own pain."[7]

In a universal key, lament might be addressed to a god (or gods), but it might also be directed to other human hearers—whether they are fellow-sufferers, fellow humans who are invited into the lamenter's pain, or the powerful hearers who are causing the lamenter's pain. For the first two groups of hearers, lament can be a call to action, to relieve suffering or bring about justice. The third group of hearers (the powerful) receives lament as a challenge, as a protest against them.

Laments are often communally shared, even if they arise from an individual pain. The lament psalms of Israel were part of the public liturgy; they were chanted or sung together by the community. African slaves sang the spirituals in defiant groups. After 9/11, communities gathered in churches, synagogues, mosques, and other public spaces to pray and grieve together.

Some of these community laments are prayers or songs or public litanies. At other times, they can even take embodied form. In chapter 1, I briefly explored how some of the healing stories in the Gospels might be considered embodied enactments of lament. People cry out to Jesus for help and healing, and he responds with compassion—restoring their sight, restoring them to their communities,

---

7. Billman and Migliore, *Rachel's Cry*, 123.

forgiving their sins. Some public protests might be considered a form of embodied lament in a universal key.

For example, in 2003, Christian and Muslim women repeatedly staged silent protests outside the Liberian presidential palace to demand a peaceful end to the violent conflict between the warlords and Charles Taylor's government. They wore white T-shirts as a sign of their solidarity. When peace talks stalled, they blockaded the men into the negotiating room and threatened to remove their clothes to shame the men into action.[8]

In South America, the Madres de Plaza de Mayo (the Mothers of the Plaza de Mayo) were mothers and grandmothers who stood vigil for almost thirty years, from 1977 to 2006, on behalf of the victims who had been "disappeared" during the military dictatorship in Argentina.

In South Africa, the women of the Black Sash movement gathered for over forty years to protest apartheid. They stood silently in public places wearing black sashes as visible signs of protest. As white women, they stood in solidarity with the suffering of their black African sisters (*weep with those who weep*). Like the white T-shirts of the Liberian women, like the sackcloth and ashes of ancient Israel, the black sashes bore visible witness to their protesting laments, even though they never spoke.

In all these examples, the lamenters are women. It's possible that women use embodied laments as a form of protest because other avenues of power are so often closed to them. Women around the world may not always have access to political power, or to higher education, or to military might—but they have their bodies. They have their laments, made visible, as protests against the way things are.

8. The story is recorded in organizer Leymah Gbowee's memoir, *Mighty Be Our Powers*, and in the documentary *Pray the Devil Back to Hell.*

Their silent protests show how lament often "presses beyond itself, toward change."[9] Lament hopes for change; it is bold even to expect change, both in this life (the now) and the next (the not yet). Hearing or overhearing a lament not only draws attention to suffering and invites us to weep with the suffering, it challenges us to act in ways that might end that suffering.

None of these are explicitly Christian laments. But as universal human laments, they echo the longing of Christian lament for the wiping away of all tears someday. They imagine a world now in which there might be less tears.

Lament Against Enemies

Some protest laments are so outraged at injustice that they curse their enemies, or ask God to destroy them. These are sometimes called the cursing psalms. The fancy name for them is the imprecatory psalms (an imprecation being the formal word for a spoken curse). Rage is the primary emotion in these psalms. As is so often the case, what lies underneath the anger is even more primary: a deep and profound wounding.

Perhaps the most jagged cursing psalm in all of Scripture is a psalm sung by refugees and exiles, far away from home and in anguish over all their losses—children slaughtered, homes destroyed, their sacred house of worship desecrated and burned.

> By the rivers of Babylon we sat and wept
>   when we remembered Zion.
> There on the poplars
>   we hung our harps,
> for there our captors asked us for songs,

9. Sölle, *Suffering*, 72.

our tormentors demanded songs of joy;
they said, "Sing us one of the songs of Zion!"

How can we sing the songs of the LORD
  while in a foreign land?
If I forget you, Jerusalem,
  may my right hand forget its skill.
May my tongue cling to the roof of my mouth
  if I do not remember you,
if I do not consider Jerusalem
  my highest joy.

Remember, LORD, what the Edomites did
  on the day Jerusalem fell.
"Tear it down," they cried,
  "tear it down to its foundations!"
Daughter Babylon, you devastator,[10]
  happy is the one who repays you
  according to what you have done to us.
Happy is the one who seizes your infants
  and dashes them against the rocks. (Psalm 137)

It's a breathtaking psalm, capturing the profound grief of war refugees, and their fury at the violent empire that destroyed without mercy their lives and loves. The last line unearths a bleak truth, an "eye for an eye" plea: this is an imprecation spoken by those who had witnessed their own little ones being dashed against rocks.

The cursing psalms present a problem to Christian thought. Jesus instructed his followers to love their enemies, and to bless whoever curses them (Matt 5:38–48; Luke 6:27–36). That seems to rule out cursing them, or

10. The NIV rendering is "doomed to destruction"; the phrase "you devastator" is from the NRSV.

asking God to wipe them out. For some Christians, that has meant not praying these psalms at all.

For others, it has meant praying them only against symbolic enemies like violence or injustice and never against other human beings.[11] Bob Ekblad describes reading the lament psalms, including the angry cursing psalms, with men and women who are incarcerated. He observes, "The rawness of emotion and reckless pleas and the graphic description of hardship make these prayers credible to those who are submerged in difficulties. The psalms articulate cries for help, feelings of abandonment, and confession of sins with language that desperate people can relate to."[12] The laments "use language and images that evoke their life situations of oppression."[13] When the lament psalms cry out about oppressors, people who are marginalized can often imagine concrete faces and institutions who might fall into those categories.

But Ekblad also talks about reading Jesus' teachings about loving enemies, and "how the Scriptures distinguish between spiritual forces and people."[14] On the one hand, Jesus asked God to forgive even the people who betrayed and crucified him. He could have called down legions of angels to defend him when he is arrested, but he did not. He turned the other cheek and asked his followers to do likewise. After one of his closest friends lied and pretended that he never even knew him, Jesus gently restored him, allowing him to reverse his denials, one by one, with declarations of love instead—and then charged him to take care of the rest of his followers (John 21:15–17).

---

11. E.g., Zenger, *God of Vengeance?* and Merrill, *Psalms for Praying.*

12. Ekblad, *Reading the Bible with the Damned,* 129.

13. Ekblad, *Reading the Bible with the Damned,* 129.

14. Ekblad, *Reading the Bible with the Damned,* 139.

At the same time, the risen Jesus will destroy "all dominion, authority, and power" before handing over the kingdom to the Father (1 Cor 15:24). In the end, God will destroy all God's enemies: evil, injustice, and last of all death (1 Cor 15:25–26). In one of the tersest lines in Scripture, the apostle Paul informs the Christians in Rome, "The God of peace will soon crush Satan under your feet" (Rom 16:20).

Ekblad concludes, "We wrap up our discussion [of the cursing psalms] by talking about how we can pray psalms against enemies most beneficially by trying to separate in our minds the human beings (INS agents, prosecutors, drug task force informants, etc.) from the deeper spiritual force that they may represent to us (discrimination, the law). Jesus teaches us to pray for and love our flesh-and-blood enemies even as we cry out to God to combat the deeper spiritual enemies."[15]

David Taylor also offers several helpful insights for understanding the cursing psalms. First, they are about God and God's justice.[16] That is to say, they're not mainly about the enemies. Even the cursing psalms are prayers, because they're directed to God. It is God's character that is at stake whenever people are oppressed. If God desires people to be truthful, and kind, and just (as Scripture says God does), then why do the liars and the vicious and the wicked triumph? Would a Creator who called the world into being and declared it good abandon that world to chaos? In a fierce, accusing lament, Job protests, "Your hands fashioned me and made me, and now you turn and destroy me" (Job 10:8 NRSV).

Taylor observes, "When violence is done against human creatures made in the image of God, then . . . that divine image is susceptible to defacement. When human

15. Ekblad, *Reading the Bible with the Damned,* 140.

16. Taylor, *Open and Unafraid,* 84–85.

community is ruptured by injustice, then the purposes of the Holy Trinity are jeopardized. When tribe slaughters tribe and nation wars against nation, then the God who made every tribe and nation will need to step in and save what is his." As Job recognized, "When damage comes to creation, then the Creator's work is threatened."[17]

John Calvin understood psalms like Ps 137 as a prophetic witness to God's "avenging justice."[18] They're a sign that God does judge evil and hold evildoers to account for their murderous actions. The "hyperbolic" and even "profane" language of the cursing psalms highlights "the shocking violation of the good order of God's world."[19] When the violation is so profound, only such powerful language will do.

Finally, Taylor suggests that the cursing palms can "point the way to healing."[20] Scripture is very clear that vengeance belongs to God and not to people (Deut 32:35; Ps 94:1; Isa 63:4; Rom 12:19; Heb 10:30).[21] So raging before God can be a way of placing vengeance into God's hands rather than clinging to it ourselves.

Miroslav Volf, a native Croatian, writes out of his experience during the Balkan war that tore apart ethnic Croats (predominantly Catholic), ethnic Serbs (predominantly Orthodox), Muslims, and Jews in the former Yugoslavia. As a Croat, he wrestled with whether he could "embrace" one of the Serbian fighters who "had been sowing desolation in my native country, herding people into concentration camps, raping women, burning down

---

17. Taylor, *Open and Unafraid*, 85.

18. Calvin, *Commentary on the Book of Psalms*, 196.

19. Taylor, *Open and Unafraid*, 86.

20. Taylor, *Open and Unafraid*, 88.

21. See Brueggemann, *Praying the Psalms*, 70–73.

churches, and destroying cities."[22] For Volf, "embrace" refers to "God's reception of hostile humanity into divine communion" as the model for how human beings should relate to the hated other, to even their enemies. The movement from excluding enemies to embracing them involves repentance, forgiveness, "making space in oneself for the other" (as God makes space for God's enemies through the cross), and the "healing of memory."[23]

Volf knows that the obstacles in the path toward forgiveness can seem insurmountable. He invokes the cursing psalms to suggest that placing our rage before God can help us find "a way out of slavery to revenge and into the freedom of forgiveness."[24] He continues, "by placing unattended rage before God we place both our unjust enemy and our own vengeful self face to face with a God who loves and does justice."[25]

This isn't to say that the cursing psalms—and this type of lament more broadly—don't have dangers. The cursing psalms have been misused in the past as anti-Jewish polemic, and they can provide convenient vehicles for uncritically identifying and condemning present-day enemies.[26]

Even more so than other laments, the cursing psalms arise from situations of profound suffering, destruction, and loss, like the vicious siege and destruction of Jerusalem, or like the war in the Balkans. A Syrian refugee or a Nigerian Christian or a Rohingya Muslim might need this kind of lament more than I do. During a study of Ps 137 with a small group in a congregation, one participant said,

22. Volf, *Exclusion and Embrace*, 9.

23. Volf, *Exclusion and Embrace*, 100.

24. Volf, *Exclusion and Embrace*, 123. See also Taylor, "Why the Whole Church Needs Psalm 137."

25. Volf, *Exclusion and Embrace*, 124.

26. See Thompson, *Reading the Bible with the Dead*, 68–70.

"I hope I never need this prayer, but if I ever do, I'm glad to know it's there."

For this reason, I hesitate to suggest that they should be used to rail against smaller things. For C. S. Lewis, the Babylonian babies of Ps 137 are our own petty resentments.[27] This could be a helpful way to reorient the cursing psalms away from fury toward other human beings and toward our own failures—making them in essence penitential prayers instead of protest songs. At the same time, I'm not sure this does justice to the context of the cursing psalms. It might reduce and domesticate them. The small inconveniences and failures of our lives are worth lamenting, but I'm not sure they're worth cursing.

There is one prayer in the New Testament that sounds a lot like a cursing psalm. It's a lament in the book of Revelation, the last book in the Bible. It was probably written at the end of the first century under the reign of Domitian, when scattered persecutions against Christians were taking place across the Roman empire. In one of the prophetic visions recorded in the book, the author of the book sees the souls of the martyrs who had been slain because of their unwillingness to renounce or compromise their faith.

The martyrs lament in a loud voice, asking, "How long, Sovereign Lord, holy and true, until you judge the inhabitants of the earth and avenge our blood?" (Rev 6:10). The words *How long?* appear over and over again in the lament psalms. Their petition is simple: they ask God to judge "the inhabitants of the earth" (in Revelation, this phrase is a frequent shorthand for people deceived by the power of the "beast" who symbolized the Roman emperors) and to avenge the martyrs' deaths.

God doesn't respond directly to their plea at this point. They are given white robes (see Rev 7:14) and told

27. Lewis, *Reflections on the Psalms*, 136.

to wait a little while longer. One scholar proposes that the book of Revelation contains a movement from lament to God's response—judgment on the violent dominion of the Roman empire—and ultimately to praise, culminating in the vision of the new creation and the healing of the nations. Revelation as a whole thus has "the tone of a lament prayer as the unfolding vision moves from a cry in the midst of suffering to a shout of triumph as God answers the prayer of lament."[28]

CONCLUSION

I hope this chapter has made it clear that I think both strands—penitence and protest—are important. Laments over both sin and suffering have a place. I've highlighted the protest strand because it tends to be more muted in most Christian traditions. Over time, lament as penitence for sin became the dominant stream of lament practiced in Christian worship and liturgy.

Lament today remains a vibrant strand of Jewish life in the modern era, especially in relation to the suffering of the Shoah (the Holocaust).[29] Recently, some Christians have made a case for the value of lament in private and public life, in worship and in the public square. Old Testament scholar Walter Brueggemann has long been one of the most prominent advocates for lament. Other recent voices include Scott Ellington, Kathleen Billman, and Daniel Migliore.[30] I add my voice to that small and growing chorus here.

28. Ellington, *Risking Truth*, 172.

29. See, e.g., Berkovits, *With God in Hell*.

30. Brueggemann, *Spirituality of the Psalms*; Ellington, *Risking Truth*; Billman and Migliore, *Rachel's Cry*. See also the essays in Brown and Miller, *Lament*.

REFLECTION

1. Which "stream" of lament do you resonate more with: protest or penitence?

2. What are some possible reasons that explain why Christian traditions have been more comfortable with penitential laments and less welcoming to protest laments?

3. Should the cursing psalms ever be prayed, and if so, in what circumstances?

5

LORD, TEACH US HOW TO MOURN

"... mourn with those who mourn ..." (Rom 12:15)

THE ABSENCE OF LAMENT

SOONG-CHAN RAH SAYS IT bluntly: "The American church avoids lament."[1] Canadian and Western European theologians have made similar critiques of their respective contexts.[2] Ugandan theologian Emmanuel Katongole worries likewise that "worship in African churches is increasingly dominated by 'songs of praise.' Like their brothers and sisters in the West, African Christians are now more likely, in [Walter] Brueggemann's words, to 'sing songs of orientation in a world increasingly experienced as disoriented.'"[3]

1. Rah, *Prophetic Lament*, 22.
2. E.g., Hall, *Lighten Our Darkness*.
3. Katongole, *Born from Lament*, 182.

In general, church worship services offer few opportunities for corporate lament. Lectionaries (assigned readings from Scripture for every Sunday of the year) include the penitential psalms but tend to avoid the other lament psalms. Likewise, liturgies (set orders of worship for local churches) often include penitential laments that invite people to confess individual sins, especially during the season of Lent, but they tend to exclude laments of suffering or protest.

The cursing psalms discussed in chapter 4 almost never appear in lectionaries or liturgies. There are some good reasons for that omission—the cursing psalms are easily misused—but this absence contributes to a sense that anger is not an appropriate emotion in church. It surely makes it hard to express anger or frustration to God, even when people may be feeling those things.

The situation is no better in "low-church" worship services that don't have set liturgies or hymns. A few years ago, one study showed that only five of the top 100 worship songs frequently sung in local churches in the United States qualified as laments.[4] It's pretty normal to hear American Christians complaining that they have to put on a "happy face" to go to church, masking the real pain or chaos of their lives from their fellow worshipers.

Likewise, there are relatively few spaces for lament in the public square, in other communal gatherings. Western culture in general has no clear role for public mourning or grief. We have plenty of venues for complaint, but not for collective lament. Social media provides ample opportunities for contempt, outrage, and shaming. And it idolizes idealized celebrations—photos of artfully arranged dinner plates, happy families, perfect hair, slender bodies.

4. Rah, *Prophetic Lament*, 22.

Occasionally one will find a lament in those spaces. But not often.

Costly Losses

The losses that result from the absence of lament in churches, and other communal spaces, are many.[5] It might lead Christians to think that God covets only our praise and our penitence, but never welcomes our struggles or our griefs. This is, in my view, a skewed version of Christianity, one in which God cares more about our sin than our suffering.

Failing to authorize and invite lament pushes suffering, and those who suffer, to the margins, and in some cases out of churches altogether. Other Christians can sometimes treat struggles with faith or with suffering as signs of a weak faith or even marks of sin in a person's life (see the discussion of doubt in chapter 3). This compounds the pain and drives people away from the communities that should be functioning as a support system in times of crisis.

Clarissa Moll wrote about how hard it was to go to church again after her husband died: "Many grieving people find church one of the hardest places to return to after loss. Some find uplifting worship services jarring in the face of their grief."[6] She urges churches to incorporate lament into their regular services:

> Lament offers space for those grieving to bring their sorrows before the God who hears our cries and binds up our wounds. Lament in corporate worship also reminds the larger body that there are those among us we must carry gently, who need our comfort and care. We remind the

5. Brueggemann, "Costly Loss of Lament," 57–71; Suderman, "Cost of Losing Lament," 201–17.

6. Moll, "Letting Grief Come to Church."

> bereaved they are not forgotten; their tears mat-
> ter to God and to us.[7]

Another possible effect of excluding lament is that it cel-
ebrates and brings to the forefront those who don't currently
need lament, while failing to account for the experience of
those whose lives are filled with lament. Because lament can
be a protest against the way things are, its absence suggests
that the way things are is perfectly fine.

Especially when the sole focus is on praise and gratitude, the absence of lament tends to reaffirm the status
quo and to celebrate those who benefit from it, while those
who are crushed by the status quo are left in the shadows.[8]
This is not to say that praise and gratitude aren't good
and important. They are! I try to orient my life around
gratitude rather than resentment or anxiety. Every day I
praise my God. But naming only our blessings and not our
struggles—not our anxieties and fears—doesn't make the
struggles go away. Those things need to be brought into
the community just as much as our joys.

For those who are unemployed, or have recently lost
loved ones, or wrestle with the pain of infertility or divorce,
being invited to lament names these sorrows and presents
them before the community and before God, making them
part of the community's life. It says, *I see you.* It says, *Your
pain matters to us.* It's a form of loving our neighbors, and
of bringing the love of all our neighbors into the presence
of God. As Jesus taught, loving God cannot be separated
from loving our neighbors, and caring for their real needs
(Matt 22:34–40; Jas 2:1–17).

I hope that we can make room in our collective life,
as communities and neighborhoods and even nations, to

7. Moll, "Letting Grief Come to Church."

8. Rah, *Prophetic Lament*, 22–23.

grieve and weep together over our individual and collective losses. I know this is fraught territory. Lamenting the death of a black man shot by police, or lamenting the damage done by COVID-19, can feel like a political act, one far too easily labeled liberal or conservative, radical or fundamentalist, "us" or "them." It can be terribly difficult to hear someone else's pain without rushing to judgment. It's hard to hear an account of suffering that runs against the grain of our own experience or disrupts something we've always believed.

Be patient. Be courageous. Be willing to listen and learn from the suffering of others. Learning to lament together is an art that takes time. Sitting still in the presence of pain is not easy. Providing the structure and framework of lament can help chart a place to begin (see chapter 1).

For the examples in this chapter, I'll begin with the closest of losses—the death of a loved one—and move outward from there in widening concentric circles, to consider lament in the context of neighborhoods, communities, and nations.

JESUS LOSES A FRIEND

Death is the first context where lament has a role to play. Losing a loved one is a universal experience. Every human being, if they live long enough, goes through it eventually. It's not easy to talk about death or how to cope with its aftermath. There are many rituals that help us navigate death. Lament is one of them. I've chosen to frame this theme with the story of a death in John's Gospel, because it's a death that Jesus himself mourns.

Of the four Gospel writers, it's John who shows us Jesus' friends. In fact, it's really only in John that we see that Jesus *has* friends. In John's Gospel, Jesus calls his disciples his friends, and tells them that the greatest love anyone can have is a willingness to die for one's friends (John 15:13–15). Apart from his disciples, his closest friends are three siblings: Mary, Martha, and Lazarus of the little hill town of Bethany just east of Jerusalem. (Today, the town of Bethany bears the name of its most famous resident: it's called Al-Eizariya, "Of Lazarus.")

When Lazarus gets sick, his two sisters send word to Jesus. The message emphasizes just how close Jesus and Lazarus are: "Lord, the one you love is sick" (John 11:3). Surely they expect Jesus, with his healing powers, to rush to their side. But Jesus does not. He stays where he is for two more days, declaring, "This sickness will not end in death"—which turns out to be true (depending on how you understand the word "end"), but not quite in the way that his hearers expect. While Jesus waits, Lazarus dies.

Only then does Jesus travel to Bethany. When he arrives, Martha goes out to greet him, but Mary—perhaps too angry or hurt even to offer him a proper greeting—stays home. Eventually, both Martha and Mary will say exactly the same thing to Jesus: "Lord, if you had been here, my brother would not have died" (John 11:21, 32). It's a lament-like accusation. Jesus was human; it must have stung him to be accused of causing the death of his beloved friend (*the one you love*). When Jesus sees the sisters and the other people gathered there weeping, "he was deeply moved in spirit and troubled" (John 11:33).

When Jesus sees the tomb where his beloved friend has been laid, he weeps. (*Weep with those who weep.*) If this is a lament, it's a silent one; there's no invocation, no petition, no complaint. Just tears. Despite knowing what he is about to do, Jesus does not order the mourners to stop weeping. Instead, he participates with them in their mourning.

For theologian Karl Barth, the weeping of Jesus at the tomb of Lazarus is both a form of solidarity with suffering humanity, and "a resolute No" to the reality of death. The author and giver of life stands in "the sphere of death" and (in Barth's dramatic description) flings a powerful Yes into that sphere, a Yes that calls forth Lazarus, who emerges from the tomb still wrapped in his graveclothes.[9] Jesus stands on both sides of the lament, both the mourner and the one who hears even wordless cries of grief, both the friend who aches with loss and the One who overturns and restores all losses.

What does this have to say about how lament functions in the face of death? Over time, American funerals have gradually transitioned from rituals of mourning and grief to celebrations of the deceased person's life. Where once open caskets were common, the dead person's body is now rarely present. The impulse to celebrate certainly isn't all wrong. When my mother died, it was a comfort to remember and name all the joy and goodness she'd brought to so many lives. But I was also shocked and shattered that I'd lost my mom while I was in my thirties. At her funeral, I didn't want (mostly) to celebrate; I wanted to grieve.

Lamenting in the face of death allows us to acknowledge the awfulness of death—the way it leaves gaping holes behind—while still saying Yes to the power that does not abandon us to death.[10] Lament is not only for the funeral itself, although I think it has a central role to play in that ritual. It's also for remembering, and incorporating into our

9. Barth, *Church Dogmatics* IV/2.15, §64.3.

10. One resource for ministers is Norén, *In Times of Crisis and Sorrow*. Debbie Perlman's little book *Flames to Heaven* includes laments modeled on the scriptural psalms. See also Verhey, *Christian Art of Dying*, 216–54; and Bier and Bulkeley, *Spiritual Complaint*, especially essays by Robin Parry ("Wrestling with Lamentations in Christian Worship"), Colin Buchanan ("Liturgy and Lament"), and Jeanette Mathews ("Framing Lament: Providing a Context for the Expression of Pain").

common lives, the losses that so many continue to grieve after the funeral is over.

LAMENTING IN COMMUNITY

Lamenting together as a community means something more than just intercessory prayer. It means being willing to enter into and share pain. Lamenting in community is a form of vulnerable hospitality and a form of solidarity.

When I think of hospitable spaces, I think of my time living in Uzbekistan, a culture that places a high value on hospitality. When you enter someone's home, you take your shoes off, leaving them at the door along with the dust of the outside world. You might be offered slippers. You will definitely be offered tea and bread. You expect to stay awhile. The host does everything in her power to tend to your needs, to make you feel comfortable and welcomed. When you are a guest in someone's home, they will never harm you or show you disrespect. In the early days of the church, Christians were exhorted to show hospitality even to strangers (Matt 25:35; Heb 13:12).

Lamenting means vulnerable hospitality, because it requires us to be willing to tell our own painful stories, and to hear the painful stories of others and to be changed by them. We expect to stay awhile. We open ourselves up to the possibility of being wounded ourselves by another person's wounds. We invite others into the dark places of our lives. We go into spaces where we're willing to take off our shoes, and where we're attentive to the needs of others, and where we promise not to harm one another.

Lamenting in community also means solidarity with the hurting. Solidarity means the joys of other people are my joys. It means the griefs and anxieties of other people are also my griefs and anxieties.[11] When you celebrate, I rejoice. When you mourn, I mourn.

In the Gospel of Matthew, Jesus declares that the merciful are blessed (Matt 5:7). For the church's entire history, Christians have assumed that mercy is both an emotion (compassion) and a set of concrete actions to meet needs. For example, when Reformer John Calvin explored Jesus' blessing of the merciful, he described mercy first as suffering with the neighbor's afflictions, or what we might today call empathy: "We must assume their identity, as it were, so as to be deeply touched by their suffering and moved by love to mourn with them." Mercy, he writes, "is the grief we experience from the sadness of others."[12] But grief *by itself* is not mercy, until it is put into action—forgiving wrongs, canceling debts, meeting material needs.

Puritan preacher Jeremiah Burroughs said, "mercy causes one to put himself into the same state, to be in bonds with those that are in bonds, and to weep with those that weep."[13] Burroughs also told his congregation that they would never be moved to mercy if they didn't see suffering.[14] True mercy, the mercy of the beatitudes, has to draw close enough to *see* suffering, to weep with those who weep.

Bryan Stevenson is a lawyer who has dedicated his career to defending the poor and the wrongly condemned. He recalls his grandmother often telling him, "You can't

11. I'm borrowing a phrase from a document by Pope Paul VI called *Gaudium et Spes* (its English title is "Pastoral Constitution on the Church in the Modern World"): "The joys and the hopes, the griefs and the anxieties of the men of this age, especially those who are poor or in any way afflicted, these are the joys and hopes, the griefs and anxieties of the followers of Christ. Indeed, nothing genuinely human fails to raise an echo in their hearts" (para. 1).

12. Calvin, *Sermons on the Beatitudes*, 42, 63.

13. Burroughs, *Saints' Happiness*, 135–36.

14. Burroughs, *Saints' Happiness*, 151.

understand most of the important things from a distance, Bryan. You have to get close."[15] To lament with others, as a form of solidarity, means we need to draw near to those who suffer most. But Stevenson also resists drawing a line between those who suffer and those who help. He writes that "being broken is what makes us human. . . . Our shared vulnerability and imperfection nurtures and sustains our capacity for compassion."[16]

In the Evangelical Covenant Church (the church I call home), there's a "six-fold test" for its commitment to multiethnic ministry. The sixth test is practicing solidarity: "In what ways are we standing with and advocating for the multiethnic mosaic? How are we sharing in the suffering of others both individually and communally?"[17]

Solidarity, like lament, takes practice. Dominique Gilliard describes it as a muscle that we have to exercise.[18] It means we need to think about who counts as "my community." Which voices are included? Whose voices are absent or muted?

For white people, including white Christians, it can be difficult to learn to listen to the voices of people of color. For men, it can be hard to hear the experiences of women when we describe how we're harassed or interrupted or demeaned. For people who are straight, it can be a challenge to listen to the hurtful experiences of people who identify as gay or queer. For the privileged and wealthy, it can be hard to hear the voices of the marginalized and the poor. I'll speak for myself: it can be easy for me to use my privilege and wealth

15. Stevenson, *Just Mercy*, 14.

16. Stevenson, *Just Mercy*, 289.

17. The other five tests are population, participation, power, pace-setting, and purposeful narrative (https://covchurch.org/resources/six-fold-test/).

18. Gilliard, interview with Alex Gee.

to fence myself off from the poor, to spend my days only in places where the poor never go.

Catherine Gugerty was a long-time director of a university's community service programs. When she gives advice to college students who are about to engage in community service, she urges them to look the clients in the eye, "acknowledging his or her personhood." Ask a question and wait for an answer. Wait for them to tell their stories; be patient. Be consistent; show up reliably in their lives. And show compassion, which for her means to "suffer with."[19]

The most vulnerable are often treated as if their stories are less important. Jewish and Christian Scriptures insist that their stories are *more* important. God hears *especially* the cries of the suffering; God attends to the plight of the "orphan, widow, and the resident alien"—a trio representing the most vulnerable people in ancient societies—and is fiercely angry when people take advantage of them (Deut 10:18–19; 14:28–29; Isa 10:1–4; 58:3–10; Amos 2:6–7; 5:10–13). This approach is sometimes called "the epistemological privilege of the poor."[20]

It's a dense phrase; let's unpack it. The word "epistemological" comes from epistemology, which is the study of knowledge—how we know things, and how we come to know things. To privilege something is to pull it to the front of the line, or to put it at the top of your to-do list. Finally, in this phrase, "the poor" represents all the marginalized, vulnerable, or suffering. So, to operate using the epistemological privilege of the poor means to adopt the view that the poor know their own suffering better than those who aren't poor. It means that the marginalized know, and come to know, their own marginalized

19. Gugerty, "From Guilt to Gratitude," 479–80.

20. See Hart, *Trouble I've Seen*, 83–87.

positions more clearly than those in the mainstream. They have privileged knowledge, insider wisdom.

It means that the suffering have a clearer grasp of their pain (and what they need in the midst of their pain) than those who aren't suffering. They get to stand in the front of the line and to talk first when we ask questions about suffering, or poverty, or discrimination. Because they *know* about those things. If we're talking about sexual violence against women, or the gender pay gap, women get to step up to speak and men get to step back. If we're talking about discrimination against Asian Americans, then Asian Americans get to talk and I, as a white woman, get to listen.

Why? Because we will not know how to lament as a community until we *know* what we're lamenting about and who we're lamenting with. We have to draw near, and we have to listen. And then we can mourn with those who mourn.

Old Testament scholar Walter Brueggemann claims that a "community that regularly voices lament is a community that *acknowledges present pain* and that *anticipates transformation.*"[21] Lament not only acknowledges the pain of the present, it also looks toward the future, when things might be, could be, otherwise. Lament mourns the way things are but isn't content to let them stay that way.

Lament is a form of truth-telling, which is both an important act in itself and the starting-point to change, to breaking free. Emmanuel Katongole writes, "The anticipation is thus that seeing truly will bring us to a breaking point, to a moment of 'enough is enough,' which is the starting point for transformative agency and liberating struggle. Herein lies the power of poetic lament: it forces us to 'see'— and thus to assume responsibility and take action."[22] The

21. Brueggemann, "Lament as Wake-Up Call," 233.

22. Katongole, *Born from Lament*, 96.

goal of lament is not sorrow for sorrow's sake. The ultimate goal is restoration, transformation, healing. Lament presses in hope toward a more peaceful and just future.

Lament and Injustice

Lamenting in a community reframes lament; it becomes not only an individual practice but also a communal one. It's not only private and personal but also social and corporate. This reframing will inevitably draw attention to the wider social issues that cause suffering, whether those social forces are poverty or food deserts, domestic violence or racial profiling. In this way, lament wakes us up, or keeps us awake, "to forces of injustice."[23]

For example, one of the pains that lingers just below the surface of almost any community is domestic violence, including sexual violence. In the previous chapter, I talked about penitence and protest as the two main strands of lament. Domestic and sexual violence involve both strands. As penitence, lament is a prayer of grief and repentance for the times that churches or communities have been silent or complicit in the abuse of women and children. It could be a prayer of grief and repentance for anyone who once lifted a hand in violence against another person. As protest, lament calls on God's justice to protect the vulnerable and hold abusers to account for their actions.[24]

Another social pain that I've had to learn how to lament is the profound suffering of racial injustice that shapes the history of my country: the systematic and violent disenfranchisement of the Native American tribes, the immigration laws designed to favor people who are considered white and

23. Billman and Migliore, *Rachel's Cry*, 92.

24. For a good resource, see Michel, "Scripture Says More than Just 'Forgive,'" 17–20.

to exclude those who are not, the legacy of slavery passed down into Jim Crow laws and into the criminal justice system.[25] In the United States, it's impossible to talk about lamenting in community and not lament about racial injustice and the damage it does to all of us.

As a white Christian, for example, I'm being asked by my African-American brothers and sisters to look at their pain and not to look away. To sit still and listen. To lament in repentance for how I have been silent or complicit in a system that wounds them, to lament in protest against the structures that bind them up and beat them down.

You may already have this issue on your heart. You may already be lamenting about it; you may already be moved to action. But if not, here are some good places to begin learning about racial justice in the context of Christianity, including the role of lament:

- Drew Hart, *Trouble I've Seen*

- Soong-Chan Rah, *Prophetic Lament*

- Chanequa Walker-Barnes, *I Bring the Voices of My People*

- Dominique Gilliard, *Rethinking Incarceration*

The problem of social injustices can be paralyzing. I often feel overwhelmed and unsure how to respond. Lament is one response. It's not the only response, but it's an important one. It can be a first step. Emanuel Katongole and Chris Rice argue that lament is the first step on the way toward racial reconciliation (or racial justice, as some prefer to call it). But they also suggest that we need to *learn* how to lament. For them, lament is "the prayer of those

25. For a thoughtful exploration of the American criminal justice system from a Christian perspective, see Gilliard, *Rethinking Incarceration*.

who are deeply disturbed by the way things are."[26] As a Christian prayer, lament is the longing for God's wholeness in a broken world.

If we don't know what else to do, we can lament our sense of confusion or helplessness. From whatever our social location is, once we look together at the pain of Native Americans, or Chinese Americans, or women who are too often abused and too rarely believed, if we look at the pain and have the strength not to look away, we can begin to lament the pain that we see.

When one part of the body is in pain, the whole thing is in pain (Rom 12:15; 1 Cor 12:26). As a white person, I need to hear the pain of my Asian brothers and sisters when they describe what it was like to face discrimination, fear, and even hatred for being Asian in the wake of the coronavirus pandemic. I need to hear the terror of my black sisters and brothers who have to teach their children how to behave in public, so they won't be suspected or feared or arrested or even shot because of their black skin. These are things that belong in church, in our collective prayers and petitions, in the lives we live before our neighbor and before our God.

LAMENTING WITH THE LAMENTS OF SCRIPTURE

I've seen moving examples of newly written laments for a variety of situations. Douglas Kaine McKelvey's lovely little book *Every Moment Holy* includes, among other laments, a prayer "for those facing the slow loss of memory" and a litany for "the death of a dream." The liturgy "for those who have not done great things for God" ends with a series of lamenting questions:

26. Katongole and Rice, *Reconciling All Things*, 78.

Was it wrong that I should even desire
to do great things for you, Jesus? . . .
   Do I need more faith?
   More righteousness?
   More of your Spirit?
Or have you simply judged me unworthy of your
service?
Where, O Lord, do I go from here?

Like the end of Lamentations, this lament ends on an uncertain note, on a note of complaint and not praise. The liturgy then gives this instruction:

A MOMENT OF SILENCE IS KEPT,

FOR THIS IS A GRIEF THAT, ONCE EXPRESSED,

SHOULD BE ALLOWED TO FINISH ITS HOLLOWING WORK.

Only then does the liturgy turn to "Part II," when an intercessor responds with words of comfort and reassurance.[27] As a lament, it knows the turn to trust: but it also knows not to rush there too quickly.

The laments of Scripture can also provide a beginning place, or a springboard, for modern-day laments. In April 2015, shortly after a young man named Freddie Gray died after being transported in a police van in Baltimore, and in the wake of the uprising that followed in the city streets, I was filled with anger and pain for the city that I loved. I found in the prophet Habakkuk a companion who also lamented over violence: "O LORD, how long shall I cry for help, and you will not listen? Or cry to you 'Violence!' and you will not save?" (Hab 1:2).

I used Habakkuk's words to write a lament for Baltimore. "How long must we endure police brutality? How long must we watch the city fail our children and our public

27. McKelvey, *Every Moment Holy*, 205.

schools? How long must we watch our young black men go to jail instead of college?"[28] It wasn't the only thing I did. I went to a protest. I gave money to a community organization. I gathered with black and white Christians in my church to sing and weep and pray. But lament was the first thing I did, when for awhile it was the only thing I could do.

When another young black man named Ahmaud Arbery was shot and killed by two white men while jogging in a white neighborhood near his home, leaders in the Evangelical Covenant Church used the words of a lament psalm, Ps 13, to cry out in lament for Ahmaud:

> O Lord, we come before your throne in excruciating pain and immense sorrow. We cry out echoing the psalmist, asking, "How long, LORD? Will you forget me forever? How long will you hide your face from me? How long must I wrestle with my thoughts and day after day have sorrow in my heart? How long will my enemy triumph over me?" (Psalm 13:1–2). We are outraged by racial violence and overwhelmed by how frequently it is expressed in our country. Lord, many within the body of Christ, and our Covenant family, are haunted by what can feel like your silence amid unspeakable tragedy. . . .
>
> We lament that the murder of Ahmaud Arbery on February 23 is the latest of too many young, unarmed, African American men whose lives have been needlessly cut short by senseless violence. Lord, we are weary of the frequency of these deaths.
>
> We know that you are the one who brings life out of death, and that not only are you able, but that you will, in time, heal our land.[29]

---

28. Eklund, "Lament for Baltimore."

29. Wenrich et al., "Lament for Ahmaud Arbery."

Another lament written for the victims of gun violence and intended for church worship services uses the biblical figure of Rachel:

> Leader: A sound is heard in Ramah, the sound of bitter weeping. Rachel is weeping for her children. She refuses to be comforted, for they are dead.

> Assembly: We pray for the families of children who have been slain by gun violence, left to die on streets. . .

> Leader: A sound is heard in every city. Communities are weeping generationally for their children.[30]

And after 9/11, during one of the national services of public mourning, words from the book of Lamentations that were once recited over Jerusalem were read to grieve over New York City:

> How deserted lies the city,
>   once so full of people!
> How like a widow is she,
>   who once was great among the nations! (Lam 1:1)

GLOBAL LAMENTS

A global pandemic is a unique opportunity for a global lament. The novel coronavirus that began in Fall 2019 and swept through the world in 2020 brought fear, suffering, and death to almost every country on earth. The temptation to turn inward rather than outward, to cast blame rather than share resources, was and remains great. Yet if there's one thing that all humanity participates in, it's grief, it's

30. "Litany for Our Slain Children."

death, it's terror in the face of our own frailty and mortality. If there's one thing that humanity can do together, it's to weep our collective losses, to protest against the injustices that increase suffering, and to repent for however we've contributed to the suffering of others.

Thanks to the internet and social media platforms, we're more connected than ever.[31] We have more access to our collective suffering than ever before. It has not always made us kinder or more compassionate. In some ways, lament is most effective in local communities, with people with whom we have (or can build) relationships.

But when global events remind us of our common humanity and our common home—this beautiful blue globe that we all share—perhaps we can find a way to lament for and with one another. It's not too late to open our hearts to one another's pain, in solidarity and in vulnerable hospitality. No doubt there will be another global tragedy for us to lament. Perhaps, by the time you read this, there already has been. Be courageous. Sit still and listen to someone else's pain. Enter into it. Let someone enter into yours.

I yearn for the Day when we no longer need lament. Until then, we weep with those who weep. Until then, we cry out in longing for God to usher in a new age of justice and peace. Someday.

31. For reflections on lament in virtual formats, see Garner, "Lament in an Age of New Media," 228–45. For other contemporary examples, see Lee, "Biblical and Contemporary Lament."

BIBLIOGRAPHY

Allison, Dale C., Jr. *The Luminous Dusk: Finding God in the Deep, Still Places*. Grand Rapids: Eerdmans, 2006.

———. "The Magi's Angel (Matt. 2:2, 9–10)." In *Studies in Matthew: Interpretation Past and Present*, 17–41. Grand Rapids: Baker Academic, 2005.

Barth, Karl. *Church Dogmatics*. Translated by G. W. Bromiley. Edited by G. W. Bromiley and T. F. Torrance. Peabody, MA: Hendrickson, 1958, 2004.

———. *The Epistle to the Romans*. Translated by Edwyn Clement Hoskyns. Oxford: Oxford University Press, 1968.

Berkovits, Eliezer. *With God in Hell: Judaism in the Ghettos and Deathcamps*. New York: Sanhedrin, 1979.

Bier, Miriam J., and Tim Bulkeley, eds. *Spiritual Complaint: The Theology and Practice of Lament*. Eugene, OR: Pickwick, 2013.

Billman, Kathleen D., and Daniel L. Migliore. *Rachel's Cry: Prayer of Lament and Rebirth of Hope*. Cleveland: United Church, 1999.

Brown, Sally A., and Patrick D. Millers, eds. *Lament: Reclaiming Practices in Pulpit, Pew, and Public Square*. Louisville: Westminster John Knox, 2005.

Brueggemann, Walter. "Costly Loss of Lament." *Journal for the Study of the Old Testament* 11 (1986) 57–71.

———. "Lament as Wake-Up Call (Class Analysis and Historical Possibility)." In *Lamentations in Ancient and Contemporary*

Cultural Contexts, edited by Nancy C. Lee and Carleen Mandolfo, 221–36. Atlanta: Society of Biblical Literature, 2008.

———. *Praying the Psalms*. Winona, MN: Saint Mary's, 1982.

———. *Spirituality of the Psalms*. Minneapolis: Augsburg, 2002.

Burroughs, Jeremiah. *The Saints' Happiness*. Edinburgh: James Nichol, 1867; Soli Deo Gloria, 1988, 1992.

Calvin, John. *Commentary on the Book of Psalms, Vol. 4*. Translated by James Anderson. Grand Rapids: BakerBooks, 1999.

———. *A Harmony of the Gospels Matthew, Mark and Luke, Vol. 3*. Translated by A. W. Morrison. Edited by David W. Torrance and Thomas F. Torrance. Grand Rapids: Eerdmans, 1972.

———. *Sermons on the Beatitudes: Five Sermons from the Gospel Harmony, Delivered in Geneva in 1560*. Carlisle, PA: Banner of Truth Trust, 2006.

Charry, Ellen T. "May We Trust God and (Still) Lament? Can We Lament and (Still) Trust God?" In *Lament: Reclaiming Practices in Pulpit, Pew, and Public Square*, edited by Sally A. Brown and Patrick D. Miller, 95–108. Louisville: Westminster John Knox, 2005.

Cone, James H. *The Spirituals and the Blues: An Interpretation*. Maryknoll, NY: Orbis, 1972, 1991.

Dresner, Samuel H. *Rachel*. Minneapolis: Fortress, 1994.

Du Bois, W. E. B. *The Souls of Black Folk*. New York: Fawcett, 1961.

Dunn, James D. G. *Romans 1–8*. Word Biblical Commentary 38A. Nashville: Thomas Nelson, 1988.

Ebner, Martin. "Klage und Auferweckungshoffnung im Neuen Testament." In *Klage*, edited by Martin Ebner et al., 73–87. Neukirchen-Vluyn: Neukirchener Verlag, 2001.

Ekblad, Bob. *Reading the Bible with the Damned*. Louisville: Westminster John Knox, 2005.

Eklund, Rebekah. *The Beatitudes through the Ages*. Grand Rapids: Eerdmans, forthcoming, 2021.

———. *Jesus Wept: The Significance of Jesus' Laments in the New Testament*. Library of New Testament Studies 515. London: Bloomsbury, 2015.

———. "A Lament for Baltimore." *Christian Century* (May 5, 2015). http://www.christiancentury.org/blogs/archive/2015-05/lament-baltimore.

Ellington, Scott A. *Risking Truth: Reshaping the World through Prayers of Lament*. Eugene, OR: Pickwick, 2008.

Fretheim, Terence E. *The Suffering of God: An Old Testament Perspective*. Philadelphia: Fortress, 1984.

Garner, Stephen. "Lament in an Age of New Media." In *Spiritual Complaint: The Theology and Practice of Lament*, edited by Miriam J. Bier and Tim Bulkeley, 228–45. Eugene, OR: Pickwick, 2013.

Gbowee, Leymah. *Mighty Be Our Powers: How Sisterhood, Prayer, and Sex Changed a Nation at War: A Memoir*. New York: Beast, 2011.

Gilliard, Dominique. Interview with Alex Gee. https://drive.google.com/file/d/1MAvw6odZrrrMbzVCLT6m7WzxHAsAx54m/view.

————. *Rethinking Incarceration: Advocating for Justice that Restores*. Downers Grove, IL: IVP, 2018.

Ginzberg, Louis. *Legends of the Bible*. New York: Simon and Schuster, 1956.

González, Justo L. *Mañana: Christian Theology from a Hispanic Perspective*. Nashville: Abingdon, 1990.

Greene-McCreight, Kathryn. *Darkness Is My Only Companion: A Christian Response to Mental Illness*. Grand Rapids: Brazos, 2006.

Gugerty, Catherine R. "From Guilt to Gratitude: Spiritual Ministry with Persons Who Are Poor and Homeless." In *Handbook of Spirituality for Ministers, Vol. 1*, edited by R. J. Wicks, 469–82. New York: Paulist, 1995.

Hall, Douglas John. *Lighten Our Darkness: Toward an Indigenous Theology of the Cross*. Lima, OH: Academic Renewal, 2001.

Harris, Beau, and Carleen Mandolfo. "The Silent God in Lamentations." *Interpretation* 67 (2013) 133–43.

Hart, Drew G. I. *Trouble I've Seen: Changing the Way the Church Views Racism*. Harrisonburg, VA: Herald, 2016.

Katongole, Emmanuel. *Born from Lament: The Theology and Politics of Hope in Africa*. Grand Rapids: Eerdmans, 2017.

Katongole, Emmanuel, and Chris Rice. *Reconciling All Things: A Christian Vision for Justice, Peace and Healing*. Downers Grove, IL: IVP, 2008.

Kugel, James L. *The God of Old: Inside the Lost World of the Bible*. New York: Free Press, 2003.

Lane, Belden C. "Hutzpa K'lapei Shamaya: A Christian Response to the Jewish Tradition of Arguing with God." *Journal of Ecumenical Studies* 23 (1986) 567–86.

Lee, Nancy C. "Biblical and Contemporary Lament: Examples and Resources." *Teaching the Bible SBL Newsletter*. https://www.sbl-site.org/assets/pdfs/TB7_LamentContemporary_NL.pdf.

————. *Lyrics of Lament: From Tragedy to Transformation*. Minneapolis: Fortress, 2010.

L'Engle, Madeleine. *A Wind in the Door*. New York: Crosswicks, 1973.
————. *A Wrinkle in Time*. New York: Crosswicks, 1962.
Lewis, C. S. *Reflections on the Psalms*. New York: Harcourt, Brace and Company, 1958.
"A Litany for Our Slain Children." Samuel DeWitt Proctor Conference, Inc., 2014. https://covenantcompanion.com/2014/08/18/a-litany-for-our-slain-children/.
Mattison, William C., III. *Introducing Moral Theology: True Happiness and the Virtues*. Grand Rapids: Brazos, 2008.
McKelvey, Douglas Kaine. *Every Moment Holy, Vol. 1, Pocket Edition*. Nashville: Rabbit Room, 2019.
Merrill, Nan C. *Psalms for Praying: An Invitation to Wholeness*. New York: Continuum, 1996.
Michel, Jen Pollock. "Scripture Says More Than Just 'Forgive': God's Word to Victims of Sexual Violence." *Christianity Today* special issue "Heard" (2018) 17–20.
Midrash Rabbah Lamentations. Translated by A. Cohen. London: The Soncino, 1983.
Moll, Clarissa. "Letting Grief Come to Church." *Christianity Today* (2020). https://www.christianitytoday.com/pastors/2020/may-web-exclusives/letting-grief-come-to-church.html.
Muffs, Yochanan. *Love and Joy: Law, Language, and Religion in Ancient Israel*. New York: Jewish Theological Seminary of America; distributed by Harvard University Press, 1992.
Niedner, Frederick A., Jr. "Rachel's Lament." *Word and World* 22 (2002) 410–11.
Norén, Carol M. *In Times of Crisis and Sorrow: A Minister's Manual Resource Guide*. San Francisco: Jossey-Bass, 2001.
O'Day, Gail. "Surprised by Faith: Jesus and the Canaanite Woman." *Listening* 24 (Fall 1989) 290–301.
Öhler, Markus. "To Mourn, Weep, Lament and Groan: On the Heterogeneity of the New Testament's Statements on Lament." In *Evoking Lament: A Theological Discussion*, edited by Eva Harasta and Brian Brock, 150–65. London: T. & T. Clark, 2009.
Parry, Robin A. "Wrestling with Lamentations in Christian Worship." In *Spiritual Complaint: The Theology and Practice of Lament*, edited by Miriam J. Bier and Tim Bulkeley, 125–52. Eugene, OR: Pickwick, 2013.
Paul VI, Pope. *Gaudium et Spes*. December 7, 1965. http://www.vatican.va/archive/hist_councils/ii_vatican_council/documents/vat-ii_cons_19651207_gaudium-et-spes_en.html.

Perlman, Debbie. *Flames to Heaven: New Psalms for Healing and Praise.* Wilmette, IL: RadPublishers, 1998.

Rah, Soong-Chan. *Prophetic Lament: A Call for Justice in Troubled Times.* Downers Grove, IL: IVP, 2015.

Schroeder, Christoph. "'Standing in the Breach': Turning Away the Wrath of God." *Interpretation* 52 (1998) 16–23.

Sölle, Dorothee. *Suffering.* Philadelphia: Fortress, 1975.

Stern, Elsie R. "Lamentations in Seasonal Context." TheTorah.com. https://www.thetorah.com/article/lamentations-in-seasonal-context.

Stevenson, Bryan. *Just Mercy: A Story of Justice and Redemption.* New York: Spiegel and Grau, 2015.

Suderman, W. Derek. "The Cost of Losing Lament for the Community of Faith: On Brueggemann, Ecclesiology, and the Social Audience of Prayer." *Journal of Theological Interpretation* 6 (2012) 201–17.

Taylor, W. David O. *Open and Unafraid: The Psalms as a Guide to Life.* Nashville: Thomas Nelson, 2020.

————. "Why the Whole Church Needs Psalm 137, Violent Imagery and All." *Christianity Today* (September 29, 2016). https://www.christianitytoday.com/ct/2016/september-web-only/protest-song-for-syrian-refugeesand-suburban-soccer-moms.html.

Teresa, Saint. *Come Be My Light: The Private Writings of the "Saint of Calcutta."* Edited by Brian Kolodiejchuk. New York: Doubleday, 2007.

Thomas Aquinas. *Summa Theologica: Complete English Edition in Five Volumes.* Translated by Fathers of the English Dominican Province. Westminster, MD: Christian Classics, 1948.

Thompson, John Lee. *Reading the Bible with the Dead: What You can Learn from the History of Exegesis that You Can't Learn from Exegesis Alone.* Grand Rapids: Eerdmans, 2007.

Verhey, Allen. *The Christian Art of Dying: Learning from Jesus.* Grand Rapids: Eerdmans. 2011.

Volf, Miroslav. *Exclusion and Embrace: A Theological Exploration of Identity, Otherness, and Reconciliation.* Nashville: Abingdon, 1996.

Walker-Barnes, Chanequa. *I Bring the Voices of My People: A Womanist Vision for Racial Reconciliation.* Grand Rapids: Eerdmans, 2019.

Wenrich, John, et al. "Lament for Ahmaud Arbery." *Covenant Companion* (May 8, 2020). https://covenantcompanion.com/2020/05/08/lament-for-ahmaud-arbery/.

Westermann, Claus. "The Role of the Lament in the Theology of the Old Testament." *Interpretation* 28 (1974) 20–38.

Wiberg, Glen. Sermon delivered at Salem Covenant Church, 1984. In "'Pietism is the way the pastor does things': Glen Wiberg (1925–2017)." March 24, 2017. https://pietistschoolman.com/2017/03/24/rip-glen-wiberg/.

Widmer, Michael. *Moses, God, and the Dynamics of Intercessory Prayer: A Study of Exodus 32–34 and Numbers 13–14.* Tübingen: Mohr Siebeck, 2004.

Willitts, Joel. "Following the 'Man of Sorrows'—Jesus' Path toward Openheartedness: A Reflection on Embodiment and the Practice of Lament." *Bulletin of Ecclesial Theology* 3 (2016) 87–113.

Wolterstorff, Nicholas. "If God Is Good and Sovereign, Why Lament?" *Calvin Theological Journal* 36 (2001) 42–52.

————. *Lament for a Son.* Grand Rapids: Eerdmans, 1987.

Wright, N. T., and Michael F. Bird. *The New Testament in its World: An Introduction to the History, Literature, and Theology of the First Christians.* Grand Rapids: Zondervan Academic, 2019.

Zenger, Erich. *A God of Vengeance?: Understanding the Psalms of Divine Wrath.* Louisville: Westminster John Knox, 1996.